Friedrich Nietzsche [signature]

ABOUT THE AUTHOR

Ivo Frenzel was born in Bielefeld, Germany, in 1924.
He studied philosophy, sociology, and literature at the
University of Göttingen. From 1956 to 1963 he was editor
in chief of the Fischer Bücherei in Frankfurt am Main. At
present he is the publisher of Rütten & Loening in Munich.

Dr. Frenzel's works include *René Descartes* (1959)
and the volume on philosophy in the Fischer Lexikon series
(U.S. edition: Dell, 1963). He was also the editor of a
two-volume edition of Nietzsche's works, published by
Carl Hanser Verlag, Munich, in 1967. His essays and
articles have appeared in German anthologies, magazines,
and newspapers.

FRIEDRICH NIETZSCHE

AN ILLUSTRATED BIOGRAPHY

by Ivo Frenzel

Translated from the German by

Joachim Neugroschel

PEGASUS   NEW YORK

CONTENTS

1 THE EDUCATION OF A GENIUS

If a philosopher's importance is to be judged by the influence of his writings on posterity, then Friedrich Nietzsche must be regarded as the equal of Hegel, Marx, Kierkegaard, and Schopenhauer. He was one of the few great thinkers of the nineteenth century who were far ahead of their time and without whom the twentieth century would not have become what it is. The impact of Nietzsche's work was a belated one. Mentally deranged, he did not experience the growing fame of his writings; his ideas bore their amazing fruits only after his death. Measured against the influence he had, Nietzsche's life was in itself insignificant; he spent a few decades as a scholar, with something of the outsider about him from the very beginning, destined to be lonely and misunderstood. No deeds enhanced or determined the course of his life, no true honors were accorded him. Thus Nietzsche seems to be right when he says, in *Ecce Homo*: "*I am one thing, my writings are another.*" [1]

Yet the manifold interpretations of these writings range from blind devotion to fierce criticism. Pure analysis of the contents is undoubtedly possible, and has brought forth a whole series of important studies. But in Nietzsche's case, philosophical problems, which so frequently seem to lead an impersonal life of their own, can always be traced back to something personal in the writer's life. Few philosophers have been so self-involved as he was; the emphatic subjectivity of his assertions and predictions recalls that of prophets or founders of religions. The works of Aristotle, Hegel, or Kant can be understood without any biographical information. But not Nietzsche; anyone reading his books will constantly and unavoidably be confronted with highly personal and private ideas of the author's, which can be grasped only within the context of a particular situation. A knowledge of Nietzsche's life is thus an important key to comprehending his ever-changing doctrines. And the line from *Ecce Homo*, claiming a distinction between the man and his works, is merely one of those voluntary confessions which do nothing but prove how mistaken people can be about themselves. More than most great philosophers in the Western world, Nietzsche the man must be seen in conjunction with his works, because the two shed light on one another.

HOME AND PARENTS

Nietzsche's home was a stronghold of Protestant piety, his family having been Lutheran for generations. Respected, God-fearing, upright, and provincial, they embodied all the virtues and convictions of a German pastor's home—from which their most gifted descendant was to stray so far and emphatically in the course of his life. His paternal grandfather, Friedrich August Ludwig Nietzsche, had worked his way up to the high ecclesiastical position of Superintendent and had been an active man of God. In 1796, when Kant's critiques and Western free-thinking in the wake of the French revolution were frightening German minds, he wrote a book called *Gamaliel, or the Everlasting Survival of Christianity, for Instruction and Reassurance in View of the Present-day Ferment in the Theological World*; and in 1804 he entitled one of his works *Contributions to the Promotion of a Sensible Attitude toward Religion, Education, Civic Duty, and Human Life*. The concepts that the grandson was to scornfully destroy were a legacy that the grandfather considered unassailable and worth defending. After the death of his wife, who left him with seven children, he married a young widow who also came from a family of pastors. This second marriage produced three more children: two daughters (who were to play a somewhat domineering role in Nietzsche's home as Aunt Auguste and Aunt Rosalie), followed in 1813 by a son, Carl Ludwig, Nietzsche's father. As for the seven children by the first marriage, a single fact stands out: one of them grew wealthy in England and bequeathed a fortune to the family. Thanks to this, Nietzsche, though buffeted about by fate, never had to fear material hardship.

Nietzsche's father, starting out as a private tutor, soon became personal instructor to the daughter of the Duke of Altenburg; subsequently, by order of King Friedrich Wilhelm IV of Prussia, he became pastor of Röcken, near Lützen, a village in Prussian Saxony. He settled there with his two unmarried sisters: Auguste, who kept house, and Rosalie, who helped with the Christian charity organizations. Nietzsche's mother had no choice but to knuckle under to the domestic regime of her old-maid sisters-in-law. She was the youngest daughter of a country parson named Oehler, who lived in Saxon Pobles. At the time of her marriage to Carl Ludwig Nietzsche, in 1843, she was seventeen. A year later, on October 15, 1844, a son was born to the young couple, right on the birthday of the Prussian king who had been the pastor of Röcken's benefactor.

The pastor, though a lover of the arts, was also an emotional, soft-hearted man; the speech he made at his son's christening was characteristic of his sentimental leanings: "Thou blessed month of October, during which in different years all the most important events of my life have happened; what I am experiencing today is the greatest, most marvelous event of all—I am to baptize my little son. O beatific moment, o wonderful ceremony, o ineffably sacrosanct work, blessed art thou in the name of the Lord!—With a heart deeply moved I say: bring unto me my beloved child that I may dedicate it to the Lord. My son, Friedrich Wilhelm, thus shalt thou be named upon this earth, in memory of my Royal benefactor, on whose birthday thou wert born." [2]

Friedrich Wilhelm, called Friedrich, or more familiarly Fritz, was joined in 1846 by a sister, Elisabeth, and in 1848 by a brother, Joseph, who died at the age of two, soon after their father. The tragedy began in August 1848, when the father accidentally fell, contracting a brain disease to which he succumbed eleven months later. Nietzsche was only four years old when he lost his father. And thus he grew up in a domestic world dominated exclusively by women; a grandmother, two aunts, the young widow, and the boy's sister determined the atmosphere. When they had to leave the parish in April 1850, the grandmother, who always had to have her way, was probably responsible for their moving to Naumburg on the Saale river; the old lady had lived there before her marriage and could now hold court in a circle of old friends.

In spite of their uprightness, the family did not lack a certain worldliness. Nietzsche's father had a considerable talent for music; he did some composing, could improvise excellently at the piano, and was popular in court circles. Grandfather Oehler, plagued with a large family,

The house in which Nietzsche was born, Röcken near Lützen.

Am fünfzehten October, Vormittags 8ten Uhr.	Am vierundzwanzigsten October.	Friedrich Wilhelm. (Luc: 9, v 66.)	Hr Carl Ludwig Nietzsche, Pfarrer allhier.	Franziska Ernestine geb: Oehler aus Pobles, 1 Jahr Rind 3½ Mo.

Pastor Nietzsche's entry of the birth and baptism of his son in the church book.

Nietzsche's mother:
Franziska Nietzsche, née Oehler.

Nietzsche's father: Carl Ludwig Nietzsche.

loved hunting, cardplaying, and music, and was active in amateur theater groups. All in all, the family was proud of its traditions and peculiarities, and even made up a legend about itself: Aunt Auguste and Aunt Rosalie in particular would tell about an ancestor of theirs, a Polish count who had been forced to leave his homeland for religious reasons. This supposed legacy of noble and foreign blood seemed to raise the Nietzsches in their own eyes above their peasant and provincial environment. The story could not be proved, but it gave the family a sense of being different, a feeling which was soon carried over to young Fritz, never left him, and later found expression in many autobiographical statements.

THE SCHOOLBOY

Nietzsche himself has described how hard the move from the country parsonage to the crowded house in Naumburg was for him. The boy had difficulties in a new environment which he felt to be hostile. These difficulties increased when, at the grandmother's bidding, he was sent to the municipal elementary school in Naumburg. Nietzsche was a failure in the rough world of those who were supposed to be his playmates and with whom he couldn't make friends. It was only in a private school which prepared children for the grammar school attached to the cathedral that he did a little better. And it was there that he formed his first friendships, with Wilhelm Pinder and Gustav Krug, the sons of lawyers in his grandmother's circle of acquaintances. Together with them, Nietzsche entered the cathedral *Gymnasium* at the age of eight. He had no easy time of it; learning rules and conforming were basically repugnant to him. But the sensitive boy's great endowments were already revealed at that time.

The prim and artificial atmosphere of the Naumburg home with its severe religious and moral demands left its mark on young Friedrich Nietzsche; he hardly ever participated in the carefree games of other children, even then preferring to do scholarly writing in his free time. At the age of ten, he composed a motet and wrote some fifty poems. Without borrowing from other authors, he worked hard on grandiose scenes of nature and tried to make tempests and conflagrations yield to his meters. Four years later, in 1858, he prefaced his journal with an extremely precocious autobiography. Even now, these pages by the fourteen-year-old make fascinating reading; the child's chatter about his life in the family reveals a remarkable linguistic ability and is studded with self-critical thoughts of a mental clarity that herald the later Nietzsche. For example, when he talks about his attempts at poetry, at the age of ten: "This was the time in which I wrote my first poems. People usually describe scenes of nature in their early poetry. After all, every young heart is stirred by grandiose images and wants to express them in verse! Horrifying adventures at sea, tempests and fire were my initial subject matter. . . . I borrowed from no one, I could barely imagine how anyone could imitate a poet, and I molded my verses as my soul dictated them. Naturally, there were very poor lines among them, and almost every poem had parts that were linguistically rough, but I preferred this first period by far to the second one, which I will mention. It had always been my intention to write a small book and then to read it myself. This minor vanity still lingers; but at that time, I merely made plans and rarely set out to realize them. As I had no great mastery of rhyme or meter, and it always took me a long time to compose anything, I wrote unrhymed verse, and still have several of these poems. In one of them, wanting to depict the ephemeral nature of happiness, I had a wanderer slumbering beneath the ruins of Carthage. The God of dreams showed his soul the one-time happiness of the city. Then came the blows of destiny and finally—he awoke. A few of these poems are still in my possession, but not one of them contains even a spark of poetry." And a bit further on: "A mentally sterile poem, covered over with rhetoric and imagery, is like a red apple with a worm inside. Poetry should be completely free of empty phrases, because the frequent use of rhetoric is indicative of a mind incapable of creating something of its own." [3]

This personal account reveals the artificial good breeding of a well-behaved little boy raised by sanctimonious, self-righteous women who, almost like an old person, confesses to a "minor vanity which still lingers," and thereby excuses himself almost patronizingly. But there is also sensitivity, an intense faculty for observation, and a touch of that wild, imperious compulsion to create something original. And he displayed a definite relationship to music, a major patrimony, at an early age. Mozart and Haydn, Schubert, Mendelssohn, Beethoven, Bach, and Handel were the main figures in his musical education. He reacted skeptically, however, to Berlioz' or Liszt's "music of the future." Music, in fact art in general, gave the boy a sense of joy and well-being equal only to the happiness he experienced during vacations at the home of his maternal grandparents, the Oehlers of Pobles; less genteel than the family in Naumburg, they allowed him and his sister to wear old clothes and romp around wildly in the garden and the fields.

But such holiday pleasures were an exception. Nietzsche developed into a serious, pensive child, well-versed in the Bible and touchingly pious; so much so that, later on, Nietzsche could write that at the age of twelve, he had seen God in all his glory. He was indebted to the fathers of his Naumburg friends Wilhelm Pinder and Gustav Krug for things his own father, dying prematurely, had been unable to give him. The elder Pinder, who had a literary bent, introduced the boys to the works of Goethe. *Geheimrat* Krug, the privy counselor, was not only a personal friend of Mendelssohn and other musicians, but a composer himself. Nietzsche was often and gladly in both homes, and thus his exposure to music and literature was unusual for his age.

He and his two friends, Wilhelm and Gustav, together with his sister Elisabeth, formed a group of which Nietzsche was the center. Pinder, admiring Nietzsche so much that he, too, wrote an autobiography, tells of young Fritz's influence on his friends: "When he was little, he played different kinds of games which he made up himself, and this shows a keen, resourceful, and independent mind. Thus he was the leader in all the games and introduced new ways of playing them. . . ." But then again: "From the time he was an infant, he loved being alone and giving free rein to his fancy. To some extent he avoided the company of other people and sought out those places that Nature had endowed with sublime beauty." [4] And Elisabeth set down a peculiar statement Nietzsche made at Eastertime 1857, when both had received good school reports: "As soon as Fritz and I . . . were alone, he asked me whether it wasn't strange for us to be such good students and know things that other children did not know." [4]

Pinder's and Elisabeth's comments must be taken for what they are worth, but in connection with Nietzsche's autobiography they do reveal distinct peculiarities in Nietzsche's thinking and behavior as early as his childhood: the consciousness of being different and solitude (the Zarathustra motif), the intense relationship to art, difficulties in conforming, the tendency to dominate a small group of like-minded people, the fine sense of language, even the motif of the wanderer which appeared so frequently in his later life. All this was evident in the boy's earliest writings and made up his personality. Although sickly, he did so well in his studies that he was offered a scholarship to *Schulpforta*, a famous school. The fourteen-year-old left Naumburg in October 1858. His enrollment at Pforta was not merely an external change in Nietzsche's life, it rang down the curtain on his boyhood. In a later autobiography (1864), he wrote:

"I undoubtedly had splendid parents; and I am convinced that the death of an excellent father, while depriving me of paternal aid and guidance for my later life, also planted the seeds of earnestness and contemplation in my soul.

"It may have been a drawback that from then on my entire development was never supervised by a masculine eye, but that curiosity, perhaps even a thirst for learning, made me acquire the most diverse educational materials in such chaotic form as to confuse a young mind barely out of the family nest, and to jeopardize the foundations for solid knowledge. Thus, this whole period from my ninth to my fifteenth year is characterized by a veritable passion for 'universal knowledge,' as I called it; on the other hand, childhood games were not neglected, but pursued with an almost fanatic zeal, so that, for instance, I wrote little books about most of them and submitted them to my friends. Roused by extraordinary chance in my ninth year, I passionately turned to music and even immediately began composing—if one can apply this term to the efforts of an agitated child to set down on paper simultaneous and successive tones and to sing Biblical texts to a fantastic accompaniment on the piano. Similarly, I wrote terrible poems, but with great diligence. Indeed, I even drew and painted.

"By the time I came to Pforta, I had peered into most of the arts and sciences, and was interested in everything, with the exception of the far too rational science, mathematics, which I found tedious. However, I gradually developed an aversion to this desultory rambling through all areas of knowledge; I wanted to limit myself forcibly, in order to deal closely and thoroughly with special subjects." [5]

Nietzsche, who tended to be casual when it came to pedantic work on arduous details, was alert to this weakness, the complementary trait of a far-ranging mind. Schulpforta and the teachers who looked after him there encouraged his forced "limitation," and gave him a solid humanistic background in languages and literature.

SCHULPFORTA

Schulpforta, formerly a Cistercian abbey located on the river Saale, not far from Naumburg, was a venerable school with high standards. The pedagogical goals for its 200 students included not only a comprehensive background in the humanities but a shaping of the character as well; diligence, discipline, and a truly Spartan life were regarded as the fundamental virtues at the institution. The methods were rigorous, but there was no bullying; and the teachers were on the whole intelligent, understanding, and at times exceptional. Nevertheless, Nietzsche had as difficult a time adjusting as during the unhappy interim at public school; and his troubles were certainly not lessened by his homesickness, a problem that confronts most children entering a boarding-school. He studied hard, but made no new friends. The severe discipline at Pforta constricted his intellectual freedom, which he tried to recover during vacations at home by founding a small club for art and literature, "Germania," its only other members being his friends Krug and Pinder. The statutes provided that each of them contribute a monthly work to be criticized by the other members. It is worth noting that the three friends used their meager funds for a subscription to the music magazine *Zeitschrift für Musik,* which had considerable influence on Nietzsche's taste; intolerant of all non-classical music, he now became familiar with Richard Wagner. Eventually the limited treasury of the Germania club was spent on a piano score of *Tristan and Isolde.*

At long last, Nietzsche made a new friend, who was to accompany him through many years of intellectual wanderings: Paul Deussen, with whom he was confirmed on Easter Sunday 1861. In his *Reminiscences of Friedrich Nietzsche,* Deussen recalls: "As the confirmees came up to the altar, two at a time, to kneel down for the rite, Nietzsche and I, as the closest of friends, sank to our knees side by side. How well I remember the sacred, solitary mood that had possessed us in the weeks before and during our confirmation. We were perfectly willing to depart this life and join Christ, and all our thoughts, feelings, and actions were radiant with an otherwordly serenity." [6]

But shortly thereafter, Nietzsche seemed to display religious doubts; through his brilliant logical and philological training at Pforta, he was unwittingly estranged from the faith of his fathers. This change was neither a sudden rupture nor the result of any perceptible inner or outward experience. We are unaware of any spiritual torment or devastating crisis that might have brought on a collapse of faith. His doubts in, and ultimate rejection of Christianity developed gradually, as an unintended result of his education—which is why, later on, Nietzsche could rightly refer to this change as a process of calm and painless liberation. His loss of faith, probably the most crucial event of his adolescence, does not seem to be linked to any circumstance of importance in his personal life.

Next to his thorough schooling in the Classic authors, Nietzsche became intimate with Romantic literature, such as the writings of Jean-Paul Richter. But his utmost love and veneration in those years were reserved for Hölderlin, who at the time was still virtually unknown. *The Letter to a Friend, recommending that he read my favorite poet* (October 19, 1861) is excellent proof of Nietzsche's outstanding literary taste and his superior sense of quality:

"These lines (to mention only the outer form) flow from the purest and most sensitive of hearts, these lines, whose naturalness and originality eclipse the art and formal skill of Platen [a German poet], these lines, surging into a sublimely ordered diction and then dying away into tender sounds of melancholy, these lines—can't you praise them with any other word than the insipid, trivial 'well-done'? . . . But the above describes the outer form alone; allow me to add a few words on Hölderlin's intellectual richness, which you seem to regard as confusion and obscurity. Although your censure may be valid for some of the poems he wrote during his period of madness, and even the earlier ones may reveal a struggle between deep pensiveness and the gathering darkness of insanity, yet the greater number by far are faultless and priceless gems of German poetry. I need merely mention such poems as *Rückkehr in die Heimat* [*Returning Home*], *Der Gefesselte Strom* [*The Captive Torrent*], *Sonnenuntergang* [*Sunset*], *Der Blinde Sänger* [*The Blind Singer*], and I quote the closing stanzas of *Abendphantasie* [*Evening Phantasy*], an utterance of profound melancholy and desire for peace.

"The Spring is flowering in the evening sky . . .

"In other poems, especially in *Andenken* [*Memory*] and *Wanderung* [*Wandering*], the poet raises us to loftiest ideality, and we can sense that this was his native element. Finally, there are a whole set of remarkable poems in which he tells the Germans some bitter truths, which unfortunately are all too often well-founded. In *Hyperion,* too, he hurls sharp and cutting words at German 'barbarity.' Nonetheless, this horror of the way things are is compatible with deep patriotism, which Hölderlin indeed had to a high degree. What he hated in Germany was the mere expert, the philistine. . . . I only wish—and consider this the aim of my letter—that these words move you to an examination and unbiased appreciation of a poet whose name is unknown to the greater part of his nation."[7]

This passionate and stirring diction was always characteristic of Nietzsche whenever he argued his point of view. And not only did the seventeen-year-old's letter anticipate the German discovery of Hölderlin more than half a century later, it also shows Nietzsche's close affinity to the Swabian poet. An understanding for unusual language, for romantic idealism, for the fervent love behind the criticism of Germans, even for the difficulties and problems involved in the threat of insanity made Nietzsche a dedicated supporter of Hölderlin. Everything about this poet seemed to attract him and be familiar to him, and all aspects of his attitude toward Hölderlin provide clues to Nietzsche's conception of the world and himself. Hölderlin and Jean-Paul were later joined by Schopenhauer and Wagner. Nietzsche was a child of the Romantic era, and cannot be understood without its conceptions and ideas, while at the same time he brought Romanticism to its consummation and went beyond it.

In his last year at Pforta, Nietzsche wrote a long Latin paper on Theognis of Megara, intending it to be a total picture of the man and his works. This theme, which he first treated in an essay for school, fascinated him so much that he pursued it further at his university. Thus, a generally good student (except in mathematics), Nietzsche finished his years at Pforta with an excellent piece of work in the field of classical literature. In October of 1864, Nietzsche, Deussen, and several of their classmates enrolled at the University of Bonn.

BONN AND LEIPZIG

Nietzsche's two semesters at Bonn were not particularly useful; in an external sense, they brought him into contact with the university world, which was to be his world for many years. There were various reasons for his choosing Bonn, the foremost one being the international reputation of the university in the field of Classical Letters. Friedrich Wilhelm Ritschl and Otto Jahn headed the Classics department, which had produced a series of outstanding scholars. After the rigorous discipline at Pforta, Nietzsche suddenly enjoyed the finest possible freedom: he could make his own decisions about his studies. He signed up for lectures on Classics, art, ecclesiastical history, theology, and politics. In any event, he seemed destined to become a philologist through his training at Schulpforta. With the same shrewd self-criticism displayed in earlier autobiographies, he set down the following thoughts about this toward the end of his university days: "I craved something that would counterbalance my changing and restless proclivities, I craved an academic discipline that required aloof circumspection, logical coldness, and uniform work, the results of which would not instantly touch the heart. And I thought I could find all this in philology. Anyone graduating from Pforta has acquired just the necessary qualifications for it." [8]

Philology as a means of defense against one's own romantic inclina-

The house at No. 18, Weingarten in Naumburg.

[Handwritten letter in old German script, beginning "Liebe Mamma!"]

Letter to his mother written by the fifteen-year-old from Schulpforta in 1859.

Nietzsche in 1861.

Du Unfaßbarer

Noch einmal, eh ich weiterziehe
Und meine Blicke vorwärts sende,
Heb ich vereinsamt meine Hände
Zu dir empor, zu dem ich fliehe,
Dem ich in tiefster Herzenstiefe
Altäre feierlich geweiht,
Daß allezeit
Mich deine Stimme wieder riefe.

Darauf erglüht tief eingeschrieben
Das Wort: Dem unbekannten Gott:
Sein bin ich, ob ich in der Frevler Rotte
Auch bis zur Stunde bin geblieben:
Sein bin ich — und ich fühl' die Schlingen,
Die mich im Kampf darniederziehn
Und, mag ich fliehn,
Mich doch zu seinem Dienste zwingen.

Ich will dich kennen, Unbekannter,
Du tief in meine Seele Greifender,
Mein Leben wie ein Sturm Durchschweifender,
Du Unfaßbarer, mir Verwandter!
Ich will dich kennen, selbst dir dienen.

Nietzsche's poem "To an Unknown God," early autumn, 1864.

Nietzsche in 1864.

Friedrich Wilhelm Ritschl.

Nietzsche's setting of his own childhood poem "The Young Fishing-Maid," July 11, 1865.

tions—a problematic enterprise. But Nietzsche was to fail; his self-imposed philological austerity was ultimately to turn into an opposite passion.

But at the outset of his studies, Nietzsche did not desire aloof philological circumspection alone. Thoroughly aware of his difficulties in forming relationships, he was resolved to get to know and understand the world and people, whom he had known thus far only by hearsay and from books. This makes his joining *Franconia*, a university fraternity, understandable. Yet for himself as well as for his family, an explanation seemed necessary. The fraternities had already lost their distinctly political character and assumed a largely social one instead. Hence, in an almost apologetic tone, he wrote to his mother and his sister from Bonn (24/25 October, 1864):

"Well, I can see you shaking your heads and uttering cries of amazement. And my action did involve a number of amazing things, so I can't really blame you. For example, seven graduates of Schulpforta joined *Franconia*, which is to say all but two of those studying at Bonn, and some of them are in their fourth semester already. I'll name a few whom you know: Deussen, Stöckert, Haushalter, Töpelmann, Stedefeldt, Schleussner, Michael, and myself.

"Naturally, I thought the matter over most carefully and considered it virtually necessary in view of my nature. Most of us are philologists, and all of us love music. The general atmosphere in *Franconia* is very interesting, and I'm awfully fond of the senior members." [9]

The discomfort echoing in Nietzsche's use of such extraordinarily lackluster words as "interesting atmosphere" implies that Nietzsche was not all that happy about the step he had considered necessary in view of his nature. He was soon disgusted rather than attracted by the shallowness of fraternity life, although at first he obviously relished the parties and dances, as well as certain lady visitors. He also tried his hand at fencing and dueling. But it is not surprising that within a year he wrote an exceedingly polite and decorous letter of resignation. As in his Schulpforta period, he was unable to continue enjoying the pleasures of ordinary people. Later on, as a young lecturer at Basel, he was to realize this again. Even the account of his participation in the big music festival in Cologne that lasted for several days shows, despite the "inimitable enthusiasm" with which he took part in the activities, singing and drinking with the others, that he had little taste for boisterous company and tumultuous socializing. Toward the end of his first semester, he wrote to his family: "The other students consider me something of a musical authority as well as an odd fellow. . . . I'm not unpopular by any means, even though I'm a little sarcastic and supposedly satirical. I'm sure you'll find this self-description based on the views of other people not without interest. My own opinion is that the first verdict isn't true, that I'm often unhappy, moody, and like to torment not only myself but others as well." [10]

These are the words of a young man who is definitely not satisfied with himself. Not even music, at least as Nietzsche understood and cultivated it, could form a bond between him and the other *Franconia* brothers. His enjoyment of their drinking songs was only temporary. During his first few semesters, he set poems by Chamisso and Petöfi to music in a manner strongly reminiscent of Schumann.

Nor was his school work progressing too well. The lectures on theology served merely to increase his skepticism toward Christianity. At Schulpforta, Nietzsche had dismayed his family by reading Strauss's *Life of Jesus;* and this stimulus was so strong that he now became interested in research on New Testament sources. His study of Classics, however, was marred by a quarrel between his two teachers, Ritschl and Jahn, which assumed scandalous proportions within the university. As a result, Nietzsche soon made up his mind to leave Bonn at the end of his second semester and transfer to Leipzig. The fact that Ritschl had been offered a position at Leipzig may have made it even easier for Nietzsche to leave Bonn, where he had never really felt happy.

Having failed to lead the carefree life of a "normal" student on the Rhine, Nietzsche became a loner in Leipzig, concentrating much harder on his studies and thereby finding his way back to a more suitable form of existence. Under Ritschl's tutelage, the rather reserved and slightly arrogant student made noteworthy progress in his philological work. The teacher's private suggestion concerning the organization of a philological club met with Nietzsche's approval. Schoolboy longings that had led to the founding of "Germania" came true again, this time on a university level. Soon Nietzsche could give lectures to a small group. In the early part of 1866, his first in a series of lectures dealt with a new edition of the poems of Theognis of Megara. The success of his speech encouraged him to show his earlier essay on the Greek poet to his teacher. Full of praise, Ritschl recommended that he revise the manuscript for publication.

"After this, my self-esteem soared into the clouds. At noon, my friends and I took a walk in the direction of Gohlis; the weather was fine, it was sunny, and my bliss was on the tip of my tongue. Finally, at the inn, with coffee and pancakes before us, I was unable to contain myself any longer and I told my amazed and ungrudging friends what had happened. For some time I went around in delirium; this was the point at which I became a philologist; I was spurred by the thought of praise that I would reap in the course of such a career." [11]

After wasting a year at Bonn, Nietzsche was fortunate enough to find a teacher who not only had great authority but was extremely well-disposed and helpful to his pupil. Nietzsche no doubt accepted Ritschl's authority because the teacher, far from being a dry, narrow-minded specialist, had artistic leanings, and his scholarly work displayed virtuosity and a sense of aesthetic standards. This was what Nietzsche liked about the teacher responsible for the bulk of his education. In a further lecture, this time on the catalogues of Aristotelian writings, Nietzsche demonstrated a thorough knowledge of the source material. At Ritschl's suggestion, the university set up a prize for this theme and awarded it to Nietzsche for his paper, which was then printed in several consecutive issues of *Rheinisches Museum*. Subsequently, other works of his were published: his study of Theognis appeared in the same periodical, as did a manuscript of Simonides' *Ode to Danae*. Thus Nietzsche soon became well-known in his field. He had acquired the reputation of a qualified young scholar when, once more at the instigation of Ritschl, he was offered a professorship at the University of Basel in 1869, even before he had gotten his degree.

His work on the Theognis fragments did not bear philological fruit alone. Nietzsche began to understand the archaic Greek poet as an aristocrat, who had written: "From aristocrats you will learn aristocracy; but if you fraternize with the lowly, you will lose what sense you have"— an aphorism, written in the sixth century A.D., which in connection with Nietzsche reads like a prolegomenon for *Thus Spake Zarathustra* and sounds like the idea of the superman. Hence we may assume that the study of Theognis and the award-winning lecture on Aristotle (which was bound to lead to contact with Diogenes Laertios) must have aroused a philosophical inclination in Nietzsche. At the very least they made him particularly receptive to philosophical questions during this phase of his studies. However, his decisive confrontation with philosophy occurred during his first term at Leipzig, when he began reading Schopenhauer. Ritschl and philology offered him a necessary craft that was occasionally pleasurable, but often highly laborious. On the other hand, Schopenhauer's works stirred up, and gave wings to, the genius in Nietzsche. Objectively, this awakening led the student to a *Weltanschauung* based on an extremely naïve and immature appreciation of Schopenhauer's ideas.

ACQUAINTANCE WITH SCHOPENHAUER'S MAIN WORK, WITH ROHDE AND WAGNER

For Nietzsche, Wagner represented the avant-garde of music; not having read any of the great philosophers except Plato, the young student considered Schopenhauer's work the possible utterance of a modern view of the world. It was not so much the discipline of serious study as something completely personal in his nature that led to this discovery. His romantic temperament, against which he tried to marshal philology, took vengeance and became all the more vehement:

"I was at that time suspended in air, helpless, all alone with a few painful experiences and disappointments, without principles, without hope, without a single friendly memory. To build an adequate life of my own was my endeavor from morning to night. Therefore I smashed the last prop binding me to my past in Bonn; I snapped the link of that connection. In the happy seclusion of my apartment, I managed to compose myself; and when I did meet friends, they were Mushacke and Von Gersdorff, whose intentions were the same as mine.—Now just imagine the effect of reading Schopenhauer's major work in such a situation. One day, in old Rohn's second-hand bookshop, I came across this book, picked it up without knowing anything about it, and leafed through it. I don't know what demon whispered to me: 'Take it home.' I was certainly not in the habit of buying a book on the spur of the moment. At home, I threw myself into the corner of the sofa with my new treasure and gave myself up to that somber and forceful genius. Here, every line cried out renunciation, negation, resignation, here I saw a mirror reflecting the world, life, and my own heart and soul in horrifying grandeur. I looked at the entire indifferent solar eye of art, I saw sickness and recovery, exile and refuge, hell and heaven. The need for self-knowledge, for self-corrosion took violent hold of me; the restless, melancholy pages of my journal, with their pointless self-accusals and their desperate gaze toward the sanctification and metamorphosis of the total essence of man, bear witness to my transformation. Since I dragged all characteristics and all my goals before the forum of gloomy self-contempt, I was bitter, unjust, and reckless in my self-hatred. Nor did I neglect physical torment. Thus, for two weeks in a row, I forced myself to go to bed at 2 a.m. and get up at six. A nervous excitement took possession of me, and who knows to what degree of folly I might have gone, had I not yielded to the enticements of life and vanity, and to the discipline of orderly study." [12]

In Leipzig, the enticements of life and vanity were innocuous and transitory: Nietzsche fell in love with Hedwig Raabe, an actress, who was a guest artist at the Leipzig theater in the summer of 1866, and whose performances Nietzsche admired greatly. But the young man, with his difficulties in forming relationships, loved Fräulein Raabe only from a distance. His passion found utterance in a few *lieder* which he set to music himself and sent to the lady of his heart with a rapturous and affected dedication.

This episode, typical of Nietzsche's inhibited, aloof, and usually un-committed relations with women, was less important than a new friend-ship, which was to last for many years up to the time of Nietzsche's mental collapse. Erwin Rohde entered his life, a friend who did not reverentially subordinate himself to Nietzsche, but was his equal in several ways. Rohde, one year Nietzsche's junior, and a native of Ham-burg, had also studied at Bonn in the summer of 1865, visited the music festival in Cologne, and followed Ritschl to Leipzig. The two may have met at Bonn, but the friendship began in Leipzig. In Rohde's brilliant philological gifts, his temperament, and his love of controversy, which often turned into quarrelsomeness, Nietzsche found a happy counter-part to himself. The closer they became, the less they cared about other people. Nietzsche described the early phase of their friendship: "Once, in a letter to me, Rohde used an image, saying that during the last semester both of us had to a certain extent sat on dunce-stools, isolated from everyone else. This is quite correct, but it dawned on me only after the semester was over. Without meaning to, but led by a sure instinct, we spent by far the greater portion of each day together. We didn't do much work—in the philistine sense of the word—and yet we felt that we had come out ahead. This has been, so far, the only time in my life that a developing friendship had an ethical-philosophical background. Normally, people are brought together by the similarity of their studies. But our scholarly fields are quite remote from one another, our only common ground being the irony and ridicule we heaped on philological affectations and vanities. Usually we were at odds, yes, there were an unusual number of things we disagreed on. But as soon as our conversation deepened, the dissonance of opinion gave way to rich, peaceful harmony." [13]

As their studies in Leipzig drew to a close, Nietzsche and Rohde took a walking-trip to Meiningen, where the Wagnerians were putting on a festival. Wagner and Schopenhauer, those were at the time two ex-ponents of the same late Romantic world that was to form Nietzsche's entire being.

The first personal meeting with Richard Wagner came about in Leipzig, in the fall of 1868. For some time, Nietzsche had been frequenting the home of Frau Ottilie Brockhaus, Wagner's sister and the wife of Hermann Brockhaus, an Orientalist. One evening, when Wagner was visiting his sister, Nietzsche met him and wrote to Rohde:

"Before and after dinner, Wagner played all the major passages from *Meistersinger*, imitating all the voices and being quite exuberant. He is a wonderfully lively and spirited man, who talks very quickly, is highly witty, and can really amuse a gathering as private as this one was. I had a long talk with him about Schopenhauer. You can imagine how gratifying it was to hear him speak about the philosopher with totally indescribable warmth, saying how much he owes Schopenhauer, and that he is the only philosopher who understands the essence of music. Then he asked me what the professors now thought of Schopenhauer, laughed about the Philosophy Congress in Prague, and spoke of 'philosophical domestics.' He read a selection from his autobiography, which he's working on now—an awfully entertaining scene from his student days at Leipzig, of which I still cannot think without laughing; moreover, his writing is extraordinarily facile and witty." [14]

Having admired Wagner for years, Nietzsche could only regard Wagner's praise of Schopenhauer as a happy confirmation of his own ideas. Neither Plato nor Aristotle (whom the young classicist undoubtedly knew well) but the intellectual world of Arthur Schopenhauer inspired Nietzsche's passion for philosophy.

SCHOPENHAUER'S WORKS

Schopenhauer had one quality that most German professors of philosophy lack: he was a first-rate writer. His ideas and reflections seem more comprehensible at first sight than the difficult analyses of Kant and his transcendentalist-idealist successors. Very much in opposition to Kant, Schopenhauer stressed the inability of reason to recognize the real essence of things and to establish goals for mankind. Reason is at most the vehicle which can help man to attain the goals set by his will. But life in itself is not a positive value. Man will find salvation only when he can renounce his instincts, the blind work of his permanent will. Egoism is the natural attitude of man, and therefore determines his moral behavior. Hence pity is a kind of selfishness. But man is capable of his own salvation in two ways: first, through moral actions and renunciation by the will; second, through contemplation of beauty. For Schopenhauer, art is a form of universal value, but music has a

Carl von Gersdorff.

Erwin Rohde.

The "Philological Club" in Leipzig. Front row left: Nietzsche. Back row right: Erwin Rohde.

Richard Wagner.

special place among the arts; it is the immediate expression of reality and of the essence of things. It offers neither insights nor knowledge, but while it sounds, it liberates us from space, time, causality, and all finite needs. Yet the experience of beauty is never permanent, it can never free us definitively from the hardships and natural necessities of life, no more than we can save ourselves through ethical actions for the benefit of others. Only individual abstinence, total self-denial, and obliteration of the will mark the way of escape from the wretched condition of our existence. Schopenhauer's pessimism is both irrational and amoral. He sees neither progress in the possibility of rational cognition and action nor any hope in Socratic or even Christian ethics.

This pessimism fascinated Nietzsche. It appealed to the loner in him, and the aesthetic and noncommittal religious aspects fitted in with his own needs. As in the "Germania" period, Nietzsche did not hesitate to lecture to his friends, attempting to turn them into disciples of Schopenhauer. He managed to convert his sister Elisabeth, his university friends Mushacke and Von Gersdorff, and finally even Deussen. Schopenhauer called the normal, everyday human being a philistine and claimed that geniuses, a race apart, cannot help losing contact with social reality and being clumsy about natural things. For young Nietzsche, these words must have been a confirmation of his own self. And he was so intoxicated with Schopenhauer's ideas, as he understood them at the time, that he even misinterpreted Lange's *History of Materialism* as an apology for Schopenhauer's system. Lange's important work appeared in 1866, and became a forerunner of neo-Kantianism. But Nietzsche wrote to Gersdorff after reading Lange:

"**1.** The sensual world is the product of our organization.

"**2.** Our visible (physical) organs are, for all other parts of the external world, merely images of an unknown object.

"**3.** Hence, our real organization remains as unknown to us as real external things. All we ever face is the product of both of them.

". . . not only is the true essence of things, the thing itself, unknown to us, its very concept is nothing more or less than the final product of an antithesis that is stipulated by our organization, and of which we do not know whether it has any significance beyond our range of experience. Consequently, says Lange, leave the philosophers free, as long as they edify us in return. Art is free, also, from the sphere of ideas. Who can contradict a Beethoven movement, and who can accuse Raffael's Madonna of error? You see: even with this rigorous critical point of view, Schopenhauer holds his own; why, he almost grows in stature. . . . If philosophy is supposed to edify us, then I for one can't·

think of any philosopher more edifying than our Schopenhauer." [15]

Nietzsche had distorted Lange's rational criticism: the theologian's son, whose faith was destroyed through contact with strict scholarship, replaced edification through religion with edification through philosophy.

MILITARY SERVICE

Several external events took place during the Leipzig years. Mushacke went to Berlin, and Von Gersdorff to his military service in Nuremberg. Consequently, Nietzsche grew even closer to Rohde. Leipzig was afflicted by a cholera epidemic, which disturbed Nietzsche and interfered with his studies. In the fall of 1867, he had to start his one year of military service. His attempt to join a Berlin Regiment of the Guards failed. Instead, he was sent to an equestrian field artillery regiment stationed in Naumburg, and thus had the advantage of living at home. Although he never really took to military regulations, he did his best to get through the unavoidable training with good grace. In a letter to Rohde, he wrote:

"My philosophy now has a chance to be of practical use. I haven't yet felt any humiliation, but have often smiled at things that seemed to come straight out of a fairy tale. Occasionally, hidden beneath the belly of a horse, I murmur: 'Schopenhauer, help!' And when I come home exhausted and drenched with sweat, I find instant comfort in the picture on my desk, or else I open the *Parerga*, which, together with Byron, appeals to me more than ever before." [16]

But an accident while horseback-riding cut short his military training. A chest injury was slow in healing, and Nietzsche was put on sick leave until the end of his military service. A picture taken at the time shows Nietzsche wearing a uniform and holding a drawn saber. This is the conventional pose of the period for such mementos. It is the photograph of a scholar in disguise. Using his sick leave for intensive philological study, Nietzsche returned to Leipzig in the autumn of 1868, well prepared for his last semester. His studies were drawing to a close, Ritschl continued to be favorably disposed toward him, and thus Nietzsche could look forward to a solid academic career. This was not a case of "exaggerated hopes" as he explained to Rohde; but evidently he regarded his academic future as a way of life that would allow him enough leisure for his own studies and would guarantee him a politically and socially independent situation.

TEACHING AT BASEL

Nietzsche's hopes came true, and much sooner than he could have expected. In the winter of 1868/69, while Nietzsche was planning a trip to Paris with Rohde, Ritschl recommended him for the position of associate professor of classical philology at the University of Basel. The offer came while Nietzsche was in the throes of doubts as to the value of philological work. In an obvious crisis, he called his teachers, in letters to his friend, "philological vermin with mole-like burrowing, stuffed pouchy cheeks, and unseeing eyes," haunted as he was once again by the specter of the philistine. And the same sort of mood emanates from the famous lines that Nietzsche wrote to Rohde to cheer him up about their canceled trip to Paris:

"We really are the fools of Destiny; a week ago I wanted to write to you and suggest that we take up chemistry and dump philology where it belongs—in our ancestral attic. But now a devil named Destiny is luring me with a position as professor of philology." [17]

And Nietzsche couldn't resist. The official offer came in February 1869, before he even got his doctorate. But on the basis of what he had published, the University of Leipzig granted him his Ph.D. without further examination and waived all other formalities for qualification as university professor. Thus, at the age of twenty-four, Nietzsche ended his studies, becoming an associate professor overnight and a full professor a year later. On May 28, 1869, the young man gave his inaugural lecture in Basel on *Homer and Classical Philology*.

2 THE BIRTH OF TRAGEDY FROM THE SPIRIT OF ROMANTICISM

An outline of Nietzsche's life could easily be divided into decades. Between his entering Schulpforta and his last semester at Leipzig, when he could already consider himself a budding professor, there are ten years of education. He spent ten years at Basel, and after giving up teaching, he was to have a brief decade of creative work in full possession of his faculties. Even the final part of his life, marked by mental disease, did not stretch much beyond ten years. Thus the major periods can be taken in at one glance. Nevertheless, strange as they may seem at first sight, such divisions merely form external patterns. Albeit clear, they clarify nothing. For Nietzsche led a restless life, going from one extreme mood to another, torn between two poles, between ecstatic happiness and an attitude marked by skeptical, rational detachment and critical irony toward people and objects. His life in Basel, and especially his first major philosophical work, which he wrote during his initial years there, reveal these peculiarities with special clarity. Experiences and behavior of prior days were to recur in the early period at Basel.

THE YOUNG SCHOLAR

Basel, the venerable Swiss center of European humanism, gave the young professor a friendly and affectionate welcome. His colleagues as well as the old-established patrician families showed interest in him, and at first Nietzsche seems to have enjoyed the many invitations and the social hubbub. He frequently went dancing and ordered a new dress-coat from Naumburg. But his experiences were no different from earlier ones; it was hard to adjust, other people's ways of life were not to his liking, he made fun of the "philistines" in a letter to Ritschl, cared little for most of his fellow teachers, and found the noisy social whirl irksome. But more than anything, he missed his friend Rohde. Now philology gave rise to doubts, as at one time religion had. As a teacher he felt unsure of himself and misunderstood. But the experience of a hostile environment was once again counterbalanced by his sense of being chosen for a higher mission, an extraordinary destiny. All these discordant feelings were mirrored in a long letter to Rohde (late January, and February, 1870):

"Incredible how much I miss you. . . . It is a new sensation for me not to have anyone around to whom I can tell the best and worst things of life. I don't even have a colleague whom I really like. . . . The level I've reached is the most humiliating avowal of my ignorance. Working as a classical scholar and critic a thousand miles away from Greece is growing more and more impossible. I even doubt whether I'll ever become a true philologist; if I don't manage it incidentally and by chance, then I won't succeed. The trouble is: I have no model, and I'm running all the risks of a fool out on his own. . . . I'd give anything if the two of us could be together! . . . A lecture I gave on *Socrates and Tragedy* caused alarm and misunderstanding. But on the other hand this strengthened my ties to my friends in Tribschen. My hopes are thus changeable. I was deeply moved by Richard Wagner's description of what he thinks my future will be. Scholarship, art, and philosophy have grown together in me to such a point that I'm sure to give birth to centaurs." [18]

In both mood and content, this letter is typical of Nietzsche's dilemma: the sense of being an outcast and a failure and of having a mission. Nietzsche's attempts to have Rohde take his place while he himself would switch over to the position of philosophy teacher did not work out. So Rohde accepted an offer to the University of Kiel, and Nietzsche had to remain a philologist. However, he made new friends: Franz Overbeck, a young professor of ecclesiastical history, came to Basel in 1870, and the two of them rented an apartment together. A lecturer and disciple of Schopenhauer called Romundt was close to Nietzsche for a while too. And Nietzsche also became quite friendly with an older colleague whom he greatly admired and respected as much as he did Ritschl. This was Jacob Burckhardt, twenty-eight years his senior and professor of art history. In 1870, Burckhardt gave a series of lectures that gained renown under the title of *Reflections on History*. Nietzsche called him a "highly intelligent eccentric." Both men tended to be timid and unfriendly with other people, but grew to like one another because of similar aesthetic opinions and kindred ideas about Antiquity. Their relationship never went beyond the mutual respect of friendly colleagues.

BEGINNING OF NIETZSCHE'S FRIENDSHIP WITH WAGNER

Nietzsche's most important friend in this period was Richard Wagner, thirty-one years his senior, who then lived in Tribschen, near Lucerne. Nietzsche soon found the opportunity to renew their acquaintance. In May 1869, he began frequenting Cosima's unconventional home. Cosima von Bülow, wife of the conductor who was Wagner's friend, and Liszt's daughter, was not yet married to Wagner at that time. In 1866, after the death of his first wife, Wagner fled Munich because of his usual financial, political, and social difficulties, and settled in Switzerland. Cosima followed him with her children, Daniela and Blandine von Bülow, and Isolde, whom she had had by Wagner. In 1867, the couple had another daughter, Eva, and two years later a son, whom they named Siegfried.

Richard Wagner and Cosima liked the young scholar, their mutual intimacy grew rapidly, and soon Nietzsche was more or less a part of the generous household. Not only was he a welcome guest, he also received two rooms of his own, could come and go as he pleased, and visited Tribschen as often as possible. In addition to being near the musical genius he so greatly revered, he obviously enjoyed the atmosphere of this far from bourgeois family circle. And Nietzsche, who as a boy had admired Wagner's works, was now also smitten by Wagner personally:

"Furthermore, I've found a man who not only reveals to me like none other what Schopenhauer calls 'genius,' but is also totally imbued with that marvelous and fervent philosophy. He is no other than Richard Wagner. Don't believe anything you read about him in the newspapers or in the writings of musicologists, et al. No one knows him or can judge him, because the whole world exists on a different basis, and cannot feel at home in his atmosphere. He is so strongly imbued with absolute ideality, deep and moving humanity, sublime earnestness, that I feel in his presence as if I were in the presence of the divine. I've spent many days at the delightful country estate on the Vierwaldstättersee, and this wonderful nature remains new and inexhaustible." [19]

Nietzsche was dazzled and spellbound by this friendship, which offered him something like a home for the first time since his childhood. He failed to see the dark sides of Wagner, his arrogance, egotism, unscrupulousness, and extravagance. As late as 1888, shortly before his breakdown, Nietzsche raised a monument to this friendship in *Ecce Homo:* ". . . I wouldn't wish away the Tribschen days for anything in the world, days of confidence, serenity, sublime incidents—profound moments. . . . I don't know what others experienced with Wagner but no clouds ever passed over our sky." [20] Nietzsche's happy fortune in having a home lasted for nearly three years, until April 1872. Then Wagner moved to Bayreuth, but Nietzsche visited him on May 22, to attend the laying of the cornerstone for the *Festspielhaus.* The sole interruption occurred during the Franco-Prussian War. From August to October 1870, Nietzsche volunteered as a hospital attendant. By accepting a professorship at Basel, he had become a Swiss national, and the local authorities would not allow him to do active duty in the Prussian army. But as in his earlier military training period, his war service was curtailed by illness. While accompanying a convoy of wounded men, Nietzsche came down with dysentery and diphtheria. Returning to Basel after a slow recovery, he developed a skeptical attitude toward the war and Prussia's hegemony—in contrast to his previous enthusiasm. He resumed his lectures and his private work. He was not unpopular as a teacher, and in 1872, Basel showed its gratitude for his refusing an offer from the University of Greifswald by raising his yearly salary from 3000 to 4000 Swiss francs.

By his mid-twenties, Nietzsche had attained everything worth aspiring to in an academic career: he was a well-respected young scholar, whose opinions and judgment were taken seriously; he was a fairly good teacher to his pupils; he had become a full professor earlier than most, thus reaching the highest rung in the ladder; he was able to lead a largely independent life; and he had real friends. But with his unusual gifts and his nature, these favorable circumstances were merely incidental to his self-realization. The comforts of a bourgeois existence with relatively few obligations gave him the freedom to pursue his studies with leisure and to write those works which were to bring him into the most violent opposition with all bourgeois, scholarly, and philosophical convention. It wasn't his milieu that turned him into a lonely outsider and a wrathful prophet—no one forced him into this role. It was his own choice; his reaction to the scholarship and the society of his times was completely personal. The only compulsion stemmed from his own nature.

THE BIRTH OF TRAGEDY

In 1871, Nietzsche published at his own expense a paper entitled *Socrates and Greek Tragedy*. Shortly thereafter, its contents were incorporated in a treatise called *The Birth of Tragedy or Greek Culture and Pessimism*, which appeared early in 1872 and came out again two years later in a practically revised version. For the edition of 1886, Nietzsche added a preface: *Attempt at Self-Criticism*. The very dates are revealing in terms of the key position of the work. *The Birth of Tragedy* was not only a break with the traditional ideas of Classical Philology, to the dismay of all those who still expected him to produce great things in that field. But the treatise also marked the beginning of Nietzsche's individual career as a philosopher and herald of a *Weltanschauung*. It was the first formulation of insights that were to be fundamental to his entire future thinking and which he was to profess even in the closing years of his creativity, when he was working on the themes articulated in *The Will to Power*. In 1886, critically detached, he said: "Today I find the book impossible—it is poorly written, awkward, embarrassing, the imagery is hectic and confusing, there are parts that are sugary to the point of effeminacy, the rhythm is uneven, there is no logical will to clarity." [21] Nevertheless, Nietzsche still espoused the ideas; he merely regretted his former appreciation of Wagner and deplored the fact that he had not had sufficient courage to forge his own language: "What a pity that I dare not say what I had to say as a poet: I might have been able to!" [21] The strong link between *The Birth of Tragedy* and Nietzsche's entire life till then is revealed at the beginning of *Attempt at Self-Criticism:*

"Whatever may be at the root of this questionable book, it must have been a crucial and fascinating problem, and a deeply personal one as well—the proof of this is the period in which it came into being, despite which it came into being, the turbulent period of the Franco-Prussian War of 1870/71. While the thunder of the battle of Wörth boomed across Europe, the brooder and lover of puzzles whose lot it was to father this book sat in some corner of the Alps, brooding much and very puzzled, and hence greatly troubled and untroubled at once, and set down his thoughts on the Greeks—the essence of this peculiar and unapproachable book, to which this belated foreword (or afterword) is dedicated. Within a few short weeks, he himself was at the walls of Metz, still plagued by the question mark he had affixed to the supposed 'cheerful serenity' of the Greeks and their art; until at last, in that month of greatest tension, during the peace conference in Versailles,

Arthur Schopenhauer.

Nietzsche in the field artillery.

Nietzsche in 1867.

Jacob Burckhardt.

Franz Overbeck.

Wagner's house in Tribschen near Lucerne.

Cosima Wagner.

Richard Wagner, in 1867.

he made peace within himself, and gradually recovering from an illness contracted at the front, he recognized the existence within himself of *The Birth of Tragedy out of the Spirit of Music*—Out of music? Music and Tragedy? Greeks and tragic music? Greeks and the art work of pessimism? The finest, most beauteous, most envied people, with the most alluring mode of life, the Greeks? Did they of all people need tragedy? Even more art? Why Greek art? One can guess where the great question mark pertaining to the value of existence was placed. Is pessimism necessarily the sign of decline? Of decadence, failure, tired and weakened instincts? . . . Is there a pessimism of strength? Can an intellectual predilection for the difficult, horrible, evil, problematic of existence, come from exultant health and fullness of life? Can one perhaps suffer from over-fullness? Is there a seductive bravery of keen vision, that demands horror as an enemy, a worthy enemy to test its strength on?'' [22]

These last lines, conceived by a mature Nietzsche, constitute German ideology, which Spengler was to laud as the Faustian part of the German soul and which can be traced into fascism and the philosophical trend initiated by Heidegger. Furthermore, the preface shows how all the elements of Nietzsche's life are united in this book: his study of the Greeks, his love of music, and his passionate esteem for Schopenhauer. This highly subjective mixture of professional and amateur interests gave rise to that which, as Nietzsche's *Weltanschauung,* was later to acquire such enormous significance in intellectual history.

The Birth of Tragedy itself deals with a number of outwardly quite different subjects and problems. Its philological aim was to show the development of Greek tragedy from the ritual choral dance of the Dionysus cult and thereby prove the thesis that tragedy blends two dissimilar modes of life. Nietzsche tried at the same time to reinterpret classical antiquity. In addition, the study was to justify and even propagate Richard Wagner's works. Finally, Nietzsche for the first time lashed out against what he labeled the *Socratic spirit.* In opposition to it he put a new conception of human life and history, which he later always referred to as *Dionysian.*

To begin with, Nietzsche developed the concepts of the Apollonian and the Dionysian. These two terms occupy a key position in all his later ideas. To a certain extent, they may even be considered the fundamental categories of his rather unsystematic philosophy. Nietzsche starts entirely in the spirit of Schopenhauer: ''The beautiful appearance of the dream-worlds, in whose creation every human being is a complete artist is the prerequisite for all pictorial art. . . ." Apollo is experienced in the aesthetic dream-world:

"This pleasurable necessity of dream-experience was expressed by the Greeks in their Apollo; Apollo, the god of all creative powers, is also the prophetic god. Etymologically the radiant one, he is the deity of light, and rules the beautiful 'radiance' or appearance of the inner world of fantasy. The higher truth, the perfection of this state in contrast to the only partially comprehensible reality of everyday life, the deep consciousness of nature's help and healing in sleep and dreams, is simultaneously the symbolic analogue of the ability to prophesy, of the arts, which make life possible and worth living. But there is a subtle line that the dream-image must not cross in order to avoid becoming pathological—otherwise we would take appearance for crude reality; this line must not be absent from the image of Apollo; it is the discreet limitation, the freedom from rampant impulses, the wise calm of the god of sculptors. In accordance with his origin, his eye must be 'sunny'; even when flashing ill humor or wrath, the halo of the beautiful radiance is on him. And thus, what Schopenhauer said about man's enslavement in the veil of Maya (*World as Will and Idea,* I) can be applied, in an excentric sense, to Apollo: 'Like a mariner who, sitting in a boat on the raging sea, that, infinite on every side, raises and lets drop howling mountainous waves, trusts in his fragile vessel; thus each individual man sits calmly in a world of torment, relying on and trusting in the *principium individuationis.*' We might say that Apollo represents the sublimest expression of unshaking faith in that principle, and of the calm sitting of its slave; we could even call Apollo the splendid divine image of the *principium individuationis,* through whose gestures and eyes the total pleasure and wisdom of 'appearance,' together with its beauty, speak to us." [23]

However, from beneath the calm clarity of beautiful appearance, an irrational element bursts forth, when man loses confidence in the forms of perception of appearance, a loss which is called an "appalling horror."

"By adding to this horror the blissful ecstasy that emerges from the innermost depth of man, yes, of nature, when the *principium individuationis* is smashed, we can discern the essence of the Dionysian, which is best understood through an analogy to intoxication. Either under the influence of the narcotic beverage of which all primitive men and nations speak in hymns, or at the powerful approach of spring which joyously permeates all nature, the Dionysian impulses awake, and in their intensity all subjectivity fades into total self-oblivion. In medieval

Germany, growing bands of people under the sway of the same Dionysian power sang and danced their way from place to place; in these Saint John and Saint Vitus dancers we recognize the Bacchic choruses of the Greeks, which in turn go back to Asia Minor, Babylon, and the orgiastic Saka. There are people who, out of lack of experience or stupidity, label such phenomena 'popular diseases' and, aware of their own health, scoffingly or regretfully turn their backs on them. The poor souls obviously don't realize how pallid and ghostly this 'health' of theirs appears when the blazing life of Dionysian enthusiasm roars past them.

"Under the spell of the Dionysian, the bond between man and man closes again; Nature too, alienated, hostile, or enslaved, celebrates a reconciliation with her prodigal son, Man. The earth freely offers its boons, and from rocks and deserts the beasts of prey peaceably draw near. The chariot of Dionysus is covered with flowers and wreaths; the panther and the lion walk beneath his yoke. Transform Beethoven's *Ode to Joy* into a painting and do not spare your imagination when the millions sink, full of awe, into the dust; thus one comes closer to the Dionysian. Now the slave is a free man, now all the rigid, hostile boundaries that necessity, arbitrary rules, or 'impudent fads' have placed between men, are wiped out. Now, with the gospel of universal harmony, men not only feel united, reconciled, and linked with their fellow men, they are one, as if the veil of Maya had been ripped and only its shreds were still fluttering before the mysterious Primal Being. Singing and dancing, man declares himself a member of a higher togetherness; he has forgotten how to walk or speak and is about to fly dancing into the air. His gestures show the spell. As now the animals speak, milk and honey flow from the earth, so he too brings forth sounds of the supernatural; he feels like a god; exalted and enraptured, he walks like the gods he has seen in his dreams. Man is no longer an artist, he has become a work of art. The artistic power of all nature is revealed, to the blissful satisfaction of the Primal Being, in the thrills of intoxication. The noblest clay is molded, the costliest marble hewn: Man. And the chisel blows of the Dionysian world-artist are accompanied by the call of the Eleusinian mysteries: 'Millions, do ye tumble down? World, dost thou sense the Creator?' " [24]

The opposing concepts of the Apollonian and the Dionysian are gotten from aesthetic experience and characterize artistic powers. But Nietzsche stresses that these are powers bursting forth from Nature herself without the intercession of the human artist—irrational powers, therefore existing without a cause. Apollonian art embodies the principle of beauty, whereas the Dionysian never creates beautiful forms; a wild, untamable drive whose goal is self-expression, it is the prime mover of the creative process.

In Nietzsche's view, there were two art forms in early Greek civilization associated with these diverse principles, and he claims that in Attic tragedy the two were fused with one another. In Hellenic art, Dionysian ecstasy was shackled by certain Apollonian forms and thereby saved from perishing. Thus, for Nietzsche, Greek tragedy originated in the Dionysian chorus. The ecstatic choral dance, i.e. music, is the source of the tragic myth. And upon being presented on the stage, myth becomes a tragic play. The Dionysian primal experience of tragic, mythical occurrence is embodied in an Apollonian form.

Nietzsche feels that precisely the high point of Attic tragedy coincided with the birth of its greatest enemy, who ultimately destroyed it: the critical spirit of Greek enlightened philosophy, whose rationality and skepticism lacked all understanding for the dreadfulness and mystery of the tragic. In Euripides tragedy was already falsified, since Euripides was marked by the shadow of Socrates. The Socratic aporia and the scientific questioning it gave rise to—the spirit of pure analysis—are for Nietzsche the arch-enemies of all culture.

"The decline of Greek tragedy differed from that of all older related artistic genres; its death was suicide, the result of an irreconcilable conflict, a tragedy—whereas the others, grown very old, died a peaceful and beautiful death. If beautiful progeny and departing life without convulsions are in accordance with a happy state of nature, then the demise of the older genres indicates such a happy state; they declined gradually, their moribund eyes saw their finer offspring standing before them, lifting their heads boldly and impatiently. But with the death of Greek tragedy, a huge, deeply felt void was created everywhere; as once Greek sailors on a lonely isle, in the age of Tiberius, heard the devastating cry: 'Great Pan is dead,' so now a lamentation full of pain sounded throughout the Hellenic world: 'Tragedy is dead! . . .' Dionysus had already been driven from the tragic stage by a demonic power speaking through Euripides. In a certain sense, Euripides too was a mere mask; the deity speaking through him was not Dionysus, and not Apollo, but a new-born demon named Socrates. This was the new contradiction, the Dionysian and the Socratic. It caused the death of Greek tragedy." [25]

Nietzsche was convinced, however, that the Socratic eclipse of Western civilization, the shallowness brought about by a scientific conception of the world, would be superseded by a new art. Music—Richard Wagner's, of course—will be able to revive the tragic myth. It will also overcome the philistine self-justification of science and scholarship as well as the superstition of Christianity, and lead mankind to a new form of existence. This was Nietzsche's first outburst against the Christian church; in part 24 of *The Birth of Tragedy*, he calls priests and acolytes "wicked dwarfs" and sees Christianity as merely another product of the Socratic spirit. Whereas a tragic event provokes sympathy in Christian consciousness, and the idea of tragedy led the un-Christian Schopenhauer to the concept of self-denial, tragic consciousness evokes in Nietzsche joy and exultation; he takes pleasure in the power of drives, Dionysian frenzy, formless chaos as the basis of all creativity. The world has no moral justification, only an aesthetic one, and can be understood solely as an expression of Dionysus' power. This makes for a concord between Nietzsche's ideas and Richard Wagner's theory of art.

DEFEAT

It was Wagner who immediately wrote to Nietzsche: "I've never read anything finer than your book." And on January 18, 1872, two weeks after the work was published, Cosima wrote: "You've conjured up spirits that I previously believed to be only in the service of our Master." [26] In addition, Cosima's first husband, Hans von Bülow, and Nietzsche's friends Rohde, Von Gersdorff, Burckhardt, and Overbeck had good things to say about it.

Nietzsche's colleagues, however, did not. Reserve and an icy silence were the reaction of the scholarly world, which felt insulted by Nietzsche's opinions. And the young professor was soon to be made to feel this. On January 20, in a letter to Ritschl, he tried to break the silence:

"Honored Sir: You will not blame me for my astonishment at not hearing the least word from you about my most recent book, nor, I hope, for the frankness with which I express this astonishment. For this book is a kind of manifesto and demands anything but silence. It may surprise you to know what impression I expected it to make on you, my honored teacher. I thought that if anything hopeful came to pass in your life, it might be this book, hopeful for our study of Classics, hopeful for the German soul, even if a number of individuals may perish because of it." [27]

But one month earlier, Ritschl had already made the following entry in his diary: "Nietzsche's book *Birth of Tragedy* (intelligent spree)."

The *Literarisches Centralblatt* rejected Rohde's review of the book. Eventually, in May, Ulrich von Wilamowitz-Moellendorff published a 32-page attack entitled: "Philology of the Future! An Answer to Friedrich Nietzsche's *Birth of Tragedy.*" Wilamowitz, who was to become one of the greatest German philologists, was twenty-four years old at the time. A graduate of Schulpforta, he had just gotten his doctorate in Berlin. His defense of classical learning, on which Nietzsche had heaped so much derision, was decisive and ardent:

"For me, the highest concept is the development of the world in accordance with laws, life, and reason. I look up thankfully to the great intellects who, step by step, have wrested its secrets from it; admiringly, I try to approach the light of the eternally beautiful, which art and all phenomena radiate in their different ways; and in scholarship, which fills my life, I do my utmost to follow that which liberates my judgment, since I yield freely to it. And here I found the development of millenniums disavowed; the revelations of philosophy and religion were snuffed out to permit a hazy pessimism to make sweet-and-sour faces in a wasteland; the divine images of art and poetry that occupy our heavens were smashed, so that one might worship in their dust the false god Richard Wagner." [28]

And Wilamowitz attacked not only Nietzsche's philosophical conception, but his philological knowledge as well. He even claimed that Nietzsche was completely unfamiliar with pioneering studies in his field. He had read or understood Gottfried Hermann and Karl Lachmann as little as the writings of Winckelmann. Nietzsche had also confused a number of things, disregarded historical data, and erroneously assigned post-Homeric texts to the pre-Homeric period.

This spelled defeat. What good did it do that Rohde told Nietzsche it would be beneath his dignity to reply to the pamphlet? What good did it do that Wagner published an open letter in the *Norddeutsche Allgemeine Zeitung,* declaring his solidarity with Nietzsche? The composer could not come up with decisive arguments against the scholarly criticism. And so Rohde authored a learned report to Wilamowitz, *Afterphilologie (Pseudo-philology),* which appeared in October 1872. Rohde defended his friend with a massive assault on Wilamowitz, charging him with stupidity and falsehood as well as lack of respect and misrepresentation of Nietzsche's aims. In his rejoinder early in 1873, Wilamowitz claimed that at heart Rohde agreed with him, and that his assault was actually nothing but a splendid proof of his friendship for Nietzsche.

This was the official end to the feud. But Nietzsche quickly realized that victory was not his. The philologists were generally of Wilamowitz's opinion. Nietzsche was to know the consequences soon enough. He had suddenly forfeited his reputation as a philologist, and in the following semester (Winter 1872/73), the students in that field stayed away from the University of Basel. He himself remarked: "With utmost difficulty I managed to organize a course in Greek and Roman rhetoric; only two students enrolled, one of German and one of law." Although his students returned after a while, Nietzsche never managed to regain his academic reputation, a loss which greatly pained him. Ten years later he wrote: "Zarathustra is no longer a scholar." [29]

GREEK CIVILIZATION AND GERMAN CULTURE

The Birth of Tragedy had already appeared, but the storm of critical indignation described above had not yet exploded, when Nietzsche's career in Basel reached a final climax. The "Academic Society" invited him to deliver five lectures between January 16 and March 23, 1872, on The Future of Our Educational Institutions. These lectures were of twofold significance. First of all, because of the form. Having used an obscure, oracular, evocative style in The Birth of Tragedy, Nietzsche now tried his hand at the Platonic dialogue, albeit not very successfully. A philosopher, distinctly bearing Schopenhauer's traits, and a young companion, probably Nietzsche himself, are conversing on a bench near Rolandseck on the Rhine. Two young men are listening to them, one of whom is again Nietzsche, while the second could be a mixture of Krug, Pinder, Deussen, and Rohde. The latter two have hurried to the river to celebrate the anniversary of the founding of an unnamed club, which anyone familiar with Nietzsche's life can easily identify as "Germania"; the philosopher and his adept are waiting for a still more important philosopher, who never shows up. In a Rhine setting straight out of German folklore, a great debate is waged, ostensibly a dialogue on the theme of "education," but in reality an onslaught on the German Gymnasium and university. This was the only time Nietzsche ever used this dialogue form. Still very young, he may have chosen it in order to draw on the authority of an experienced intellect to back up his criticism of his senior colleagues as narrow-minded philistines. It is also worth noting that this was the first time that Nietzsche openly criticized German Kultur and drew a picture of the German spirit which showed him to be a forerunner of the nationalist ideas that played such a disastrous part in our century.

The dialogue form was not intrinsically necessary for these lectures; it was more of a tactical pretext, and it is interesting to note that the elements were taken from Nietzsche's personal experience. The actors were his idol, Schopenhauer, his friends, and of course himself. The humanistic *Gymnasium* he criticized was probably Schulpforta with its scholarly work and teaching, the Rhine setting signified Bonn, where Nietzsche had been particularly unhappy.

In their contents, the lectures went a step beyong *The Birth of Tragedy* and can be taken as a partial concretion of certain ideas only suggested in the earlier work. *The Birth of Tragedy* attacked Socrates and thus the spirit of enlightenment. *The Future of Our Educational Institutions* assailed tangible evidence of enlightenment in Nietzsche's century: disciplined scholarship and the over-specialization accompanying it. He also struck out against journalism as the form of communication of a growing industrial society.

"Division of labor in scholarship is actually striving for the same goal that religion has at times deliberately striven for: a reduction, nay, a destruction of learning. This aim may be a totally justified desire of certain religions, in accordance with their origins and history; but for scholarship, it can only lead to self-cremation. . . . In journalism . . . both tendencies coincide; expansion and reduction of learning join hands; the newspaper has replaced education, and anyone—even a scholar—making claims on education is used to leaning on that viscous class of intermediaries who cement the joints between all forms of life, all levels, all the arts and sciences, and who are as solid and dependable as a newspaper is wont to be. The journal is the culmination of the peculiar educational aims of our day; just as the journalist, the servant of the moment, has replaced the great genius, the leader for all times, the redeemer of the moment." [30]

Nietzsche's interpreters can extract any convenient shade of meaning from this. Discussions on education have never stopped condemning professional narrow-mindedness and the dangers of specialization which can obscure one's sense of the connection between all knowledge and scholarship. Nietzsche was certainly correct in his views on the danger of an enlightenment that deprives itself of its own fruits; and he was years ahead of today's criticism of the culture business, which ultimately leads to a barbaric semi-education. But his analysis, which he regarded as positive, provided an answer that was to constitute a negative component in all German ideology—the vision of a German *Geist* which would act as a panacea for an ailing time and would render possible the appearance of a charismatic leader, a *Führer*. If *The Birth of Tragedy* speculatively hinted that German culture, primarily as represented in the work of Richard Wagner, was suited to overcome the hegemony of Socratic barbarism, the second lecture already deals with the plight of education with greater candor:

"And so we abide all the more by the German *Geist*, which was revealed in the German Reformation, in German music, in the tremendous courage and rigor of German philosophy, and in the recently tested loyalty of the German soldier, giving evidence of a lasting strength alien to all mere appearance, and of which we can expect a victory over the fashionable pseudo-culture of the present! It is our hope that the true educational school will be drawn into this struggle, and that the *Gymnasium* in particular will fire the spirit of the new generation for that which is truly German. This is what the future activity of the school should be; then so-called classical learning will finally regain its natural ground and its unique point of departure." [31]

Naturally, Nietzsche opposed Hegel and the tendency of the state to encourage education by having too great a control of the institutions of learning. Increasingly aloof toward the German-Prussian state which had just been organized at Versailles, he was clear in his loathing of the "State as the lodestar of education." But like the later German nationalists, he was blind to the necessity for a pluralistic society. Diverse as they may be, Spengler's, Stefan George's, and Ernst Jünger's theories of an elite all go back to this common source:

"All education starts with the opposite of what is now praised as academic freedom, i.e. with obedience, subordination, discipline, and servitude. And just as the great leaders needed companions, those who are to be led need the leaders; thus there exists, in the order of minds, a mutual predisposition, yes, a kind of pre-stabilized harmony." [32]

This vision shows nearly all the rudiments of a Romantic world picture. All that is lacking is the concept of the *Volk* (nation, people) in opposition to the state and its fad culture. But a new facet of Nietzsche's *Weltanschauung*, complementing the ideas in *The Birth of Tragedy*, is a shifting of the argumentation from an aesthetic level to a more historical, topical one: man in history acquires greater significance, the great artist is confronted by the vision of a great man in Nietzsche's field of view. Burckhardt's influence obviously played a decisive role here. Nietzsche had heard his lectures on "Historical Greatness" and had often discussed these with him. But the image of the good old German *Geist* as holding promise for the birth of a new tragic civilization is as provincial as Nietzsche's background.

The lecture series was a great success, the cultivated bourgeoisie of Basel seeming to like the form as well as the ideas of this philosophy of education. Since at that time he was offered a professorship at Greifswald, but made up his mind to stay in Basel, the spring of 1872 was outwardly the most successful period in Nietzsche's teaching career.

The reverses afflicting him shortly thereafter as a result of the unfavorable reaction to his book, and which disqualified him as a philologist, did not shake his views. Since *The Birth of Tragedy* attacked Socrates and the spirit of scholarship, the prototype of Greek civilization probably existed not only in older Attic tragedy, but among the pre-Socratic thinkers as well. Accordingly, Nietzsche gave several lecture courses on them in 1872, 1873, and 1876, with an average of ten students attending. Martin Heidegger has also gone back to the pre-Platonic philosophers, and we can point to Nietzsche as his direct predecessor. Indeed, Nietzsche's influence on Heidegger's work in general is much stronger than may as yet have been recognized.

The nascent philosopher Nietzsche read Thales, Anaximander, Heraclitus, Parmenides, Anaxagoras, Empedocles, and Democritus, studying them in a fashion that was philosophically, if not historically, legitimate. He had them carry on a dialogue beyond the limits of history and intellectual development; he made them a small elite in the realm of pure intellect, solitary and high above the Greeks and all descendants of their tradition. Nietzsche ascertained that "other nations have saints, but the Greeks have sages. It has been rightly said that a nation is characterized not so much by its great men as by the way it recognizes and honors them. In all other eras the philosopher has been an accidental lonely wanderer in a hostile environment, either slinking along or pushing his way through with clenched fists. With the Greeks alone the philosopher was not accidental." Nietzsche felt that the examination of pre-Socratic writings was more revealing than any study of Greek history. "If we correctly interpret the total life of the Greek people, we will always find only reflections of the image that shines more brightly in its greatest geniuses." [33]

Such ideas are captivating. Their weakness, however, lies in the fact that pre-Socratic works have come down to us in fragments, and even these were added to or tampered with in later times. The longest extant work, Empedocles' *Poem on Nature,* is a fragment containing 350 lines; the original must have run to some 2000. With all due respect to the immense philological work accomplished in this field, the fact remains that the pre-Socratic fragments have led to more speculative and subjective interpretations than any other documents in the history of

G. W. F. Hegel. Steel engraving by Sichling after Sebbers.

Ulrich von Wilamowitz-
Moellendorff.

David Friedrich Strauss.

Martin Heidegger.

Also sprach Zarathustra.

Ein Buch für Alle und Keinen.

von

F. N.

Letter from Rapallo to Peter Gast, Feb. 1, 1883.

The subscript reads
(in translation):
Friedrich the Untimely.

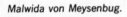

Malwida von Meysenbug.

philosophy. Thus, it was precisely these early thinkers who could strengthen Nietzsche's philosophical ego. He was less concerned with a philologically and historically accurate reconstruction of their ideas than with receiving impulses for his own views. A legitimate method, particularly for a thinker who does not regard philosophy as a demonstrable science, and all the more so for Nietzsche, who considered scholarly objectivity and disinterestedness stupid and narrow-minded. If philosophy becomes a *Weltanschauung*, the process is a subjective one, in which isolated facts and their active vital realization always take priority over the theoretical tenets of reason. Thus the problem of objective truth appears in a new light. And thus Nietzsche was being perfectly consistent when he wrote in *On Truth and Falsehood in the Supramoral Sense* (1873):

☞ "What is truth? A mobile army of metaphors, metonymies, anthropomorphisms, in short, a sum of human relations, poetically and rhetorically intensified, transferred, adorned, and which, having been in use for a long time, seem permanent, canonical, and binding to a people. Truths are illusions that are no longer thought of as such, metaphors that have lost their images and must be regarded as metal rather than as coins." [34]

As is usually the case with Nietzsche, there are two things involved here. Like Marx, Nietzsche shows a judicious understanding of the relativity and subjectivity of all our knowledge—ideas which were to play a crucial part in the sociological and philosophical discussion of epistemological problems in the next century. At the same time, as a logical consequence, truth must be seen as an illusory convention, even a binding lie in a moral sense. Nietzsche freed mankind and himself from the possibility of truth "per se." This is an essential prerequisite to his subjective thinking and to all the philosophy developing under his influence. If we disregard the more dubious effects, such an attitude is understandable as a reaction to the largely trivial progressionism of nineteenth-century science and scholarship. This was the modern, timely form of a petrified enlightenment generally subscribing to blind optimism. Nietzsche, however, set out to become an untimely philosopher.

3 NIETZSCHE IN BAYREUTH

An emphasis on the year 1872 in Nietzsche's life does not imply that any real turning point occurred. There was no one outstanding event any more than in other periods of his life; but that year is characteristic as a time of transition and extreme disquiet. Many different things coincided, accelerating Nietzsche's tendency to fragment himself and straining his weak physical constitution. It was the last year in which Nietzsche was still generally healthy. ("As of 1873, he was constantly plagued by some illness or other."—K. Jaspers.) The migraines that had begun in his childhood were still bearable, his eye trouble as well as the stomach disorders resulting from his wartime dysentery did not surpass endurance. This same year also marked Nietzsche's triumph and defeat as a professor. In the spring, Wagner moved from Tribschen to Bayreuth; the home of his friends, in which Nietzsche had been so happy, was suddenly far away—one more reason for restless voyages during vacation periods. In early April, Nietzsche seriously considered giving up his teaching position and devoting himself wholly to the Bayreuth idea by becoming a traveling lecturer. At Eastertime he went to Lake Geneva with his old friend Pinder, and a Doctor Immerman from Basel; it was there that he composed the *Manfred Meditations*. His final visit in Tribschen lasted from the 25th to the 27th of April; Wagner was already gone, and Nietzsche helped Cosima pack books, letters, and manuscripts. In the summer semester, Nietzsche gave two lecture courses: the above-mentioned one on the pre-Socratics and one on the *Choephori* of Aeschylus. And he himself attended Burck-hardt's lectures on Greek cultural history, which began on May 6. On May 22, Nietzsche was present at the laying of the cornerstone of the Bayreuth *Festspielhaus,* followed in the evening by a performance of Beethoven's *Ninth Symphony.* Von Gersdorff and Rohde accompanied him. In Bayreuth, Nietzsche met Fräulein Malwida von Meysenbug, whose hospitality he was to enjoy in Sorrento, in the autumn of 1876, when he and Wagner met for the last time. Nietzsche's sister Elisa-beth spent the entire summer in Basel. But in June, he himself went to Munich with Carl von Gersdorff and Malwida von Meysenbug, to hear Bülow conducting *Tristan.* Nietzsche was enraptured: "You have given me the sublimest artistic impression of my life," he wrote to Bülow, enclosing his *Manfred* score. Bülow was extraordinarily critical of it, and Nietzsche thanked him with impartial warmth in an astounding letter. In late July, Deussen came to Basel, but the two friends did not have a happy time together. At the end of August, Fräulein von Meysen-bug, accompanied by French friends, visited Nietzsche. In October, Nietzsche took an abortive trip to Italy, turning back in Bergamo be-cause of a sudden dislike for that country. In November he met Richard and Cosima Wagner in Strassburg. He spent the Christmas holidays with his mother and his sister in Naumburg, made music with his boyhood friend Gustav Krug, went to Weimar, where he heard *Lohengrin* for the first time, and visited Ritschl in Leipzig. These months were psychologically burdened by the scholarly attacks on *The Birth of Tragedy.* Thus he led the life of a restless wanderer, drifting around within the same limited circle of friends, a learned person, yet not a scholar, an intuitive spirit, but not a scientific worker.

THE UNTIMELY MEDITATOR ON GERMAN CULTURE

In the next few years, Nietzsche changed from a scholar of classics to a critic of his times. He had probably always been intrigued by the idea of commitment to topical matters. The Hölderlin letter of his youth contained criticism of the Germans, and the adolescent's wor-ship of the Prussian cause gave way to skepticism; but any criticism of things German was usually a reflection of profound love for what he praised as the German *Geist,* which he claimed was most obvious in German music from Bach to Wagner. But whereas his continuous study of classics had been studded infrequently with critical remarks on con-temporary matters, now the opposite was true. His isolation as a scholar since 1872 may have contributed to this change. And we must add that

Nietzsche showed no inclination to fight for his convictions in the field of classical letters; he chose a different path. The great deterioration of his health may also have played a part in this. Nietzsche's illnesses became an extremely burdensome problem from then on. Between 1873 and 1876, he wrote the four *Untimely Meditations*, which were published successively. Although far from being among his best works, they contain all the symptoms of his change and his reorientation, and can be understood totally only against a biographical background. During this time, his relationship to Richard Wagner also changed; eventually, the coolness between them led to a final break.

The first *Untimely Meditation* bore the title: *David Strauss, the Confessor and the Writer*. The opening lines have lost none of their freshness:

"Public opinion in Germany almost seems to prohibit any talk about the bad and dangerous effects of war, especially of one ending in victory; but people are all the more willing to listen to the writers who do not know any view more important than public opinion and who therefore painstakingly try to outdo one another in their praise of war and their exultant investigation of the powerful phenomenon in its effect on morals, culture, and art. For all that, let me say: a great victory is a great threat. Victory is less bearable to human nature than defeat. Yes, it seems to be easier to gain such a victory than to bear it in such a manner that no grave defeat results from it. But of all the bad consequences of the recent war with France, the worst one is probably a widespread, nay, universal misconception of public opinion and of all those whose opinions are public: the notion that German culture, too, was victorious in that struggle and must therefore be crowned with wreaths befitting such extraordinary events and triumphs. This delusion is extremely pernicious, not because it is a delusion—misconceptions can be useful and salutary—but because it could easily turn our victory into a total defeat—the defeat, even the extirpation, of the German spirit for the benefit of the 'German Reich.' " [35]

Such ideas and insights are proof of Nietzsche's greatness as a political thinker, and the factors inspiring him remain incidental. In this case, a Protestant minister was responsible—David Friedrich Strauss, who had his own way of coming to grips with the Christian faith. Nietzsche, having read his *Life of Jesus* in his youth, owed a great deal to him. After writing this violently controversial work at the age of twenty-seven, Strauss gave up theology, only to return to it later on, when he published a new version of the book: *The Life of Jesus, Adapted for the German Nation*. Young Nietzsche had been stirred and thrilled by

Strauss's destructive criticism of Christianity; but now he was angered by the minister's alternative of an *ersatz* religion. In the revised work, Strauss advocated an optimistic attitude toward life on the basis of contemporary science. The idea of a good and rational world could only irk Nietzsche, and Strauss's insufficient appreciation of Wagner heightened Nietzsche's annoyance to rage. This *Meditation* and the next one (Nietzsche's first response to the smug progressionism of the age) have no further significance. But Nietzsche's Dionysian, anti-moral, and anti-rational philosophy of life was also an attack on the Enlightenment and the tradition of European humanism.

The second *Untimely Meditation,* entitled *The Use and Abuse of History,* followed quickly in early 1874. Despite vicious criticism of Hegel and Eduard von Hartmann, "rascal of a rascal," this disquisition was on the whole subtler and less biased than the one against Strauss. Three kinds of history are elucidated: monumentalistic, antiquarian, and critical history, each of which has its particular advantages and dangers. Monumentalistic history inflames and inspires, but since it is a history of heroes, its message is only for the great men of this world or for men aspiring to greatness. But is greatness still possible today? History does not reveal the answer. Consequently, we might profit from a different approach, an antiquarian one. Yet a loving and preserving veneration of the past can be hostile to life. History cannot merely stop and observe the past respectfully, it must be allowed to smash and annul it; and this is its critical function, since everything that comes into being deserves to perish. "It would therefore be better if nothing came into being." However, even critical history has a flaw: "Since, for better or worse, we are the products of earlier generations, and thereby the products of their errors, passions, misconceptions, and even crimes, it is impossible for us to release ourselves from this chain." To find a way out, Nietzsche offers advice for a chosen few, a future elite, a first generation—which vision will absorb him more and more.

"First give me life, and out of it I'll then create a culture for you!— This is the cry of each and every one of this first generation, and each of them will recognize the others by this cry. Who will give them life?

"Neither a god nor a man, only their own youth. Set youth free and you will have released its life. For this life was merely hidden, imprisoned, it has not yet dried up or faded away—ask yourselves!

"But this unchained life is ailing and must be cured. Its disorders are many, and it is suffering from more than the memory of its chains, it is suffering—and this concerns us most of all—from the disease of history. The overabundance of history has attacked the plastic power of life, which no longer knows how to use the past as potent food. A terrible disorder, and yet! If youth did not have Nature's visionary gift, no one would recognize the disorder as such or realize that a paradise of well-being has been lost. But youth, endowed with Nature's therapeutic instincts, knows how to regain this paradise; it knows what balms and remedies to use against the historical disease, the excess of history. What are the medicines?

"Let no one be surprised, they are poisons; the antidotes to the Historical are—the Unhistorical and the Suprahistorical." [36]

The unhistorical is the power to forget, the suprahistorical is the ability to see the eternal and the constant, art and religion, as Nietzsche understood them. The man who can thereby free himself from the coercion of the past and develop a self-confident second nature may find solace in the realization that his first nature itself used to be a second one—a dissoluble product of history. This solution remains vague and unclear. Nietzsche's protest against the historical education of modern man, against being forced from one's earliest youth to dissect everything in terms of history, appears to succeed; but his objection is marred by its inapplicability. Consequently, the third *Untimely Meditation* was to give an example of a strong, unified personality as far as one could be thought possible in the present state of affairs. And thus, in the spring and summer of 1874, Nietzsche wrote *Schopenhauer as Educator*. The treatise shows that the author was still a follower and admirer of Schopenhauer, although by this time Nietzsche had probably broken away almost completely from Schopenhauer's philosophy. What attracted him about Schopenhauer and what he tried to preserve from the master of his youth was an image of the philosopher, such as he wished others to see; for him, Schopenhauer was honest, cheerful, and steadfast. Nietzsche contrasted Strauss's naïve optimism with Schopenhauer's "really cheering cheerfulness," the composure of a man who by perceiving the misery of the world had found himself. Since Nietzsche lacked such cheerfulness and steadfastness, it is understandable that his portrait of Schopenhauer has the traits of an ideal image. Moreover, this *Meditation* gave him a chance to repeat his preference for a heroic conception of history: "The heroic man is contemptuous of good or ill health, his virtues or vices, in general any measuring of anything by autistic standards; he expects nothing more from himself, and in all things he wishes to see down into this hopeless depth." [37] Yet secretly Nietzsche still nourished the hope that the man who seeks falsehood in everything and is on the trail of lies ultimately finds salvation in positive *Lebenserfahrung* (practical experience). The concrete possibility of such experience is implied rather than stated, which makes it easy for interpreters to point out Nietzsche's close kinship with Kierkegaard's or Jaspers' concept of "existential experience."

WAGNER IN THE DISTANCE

The fourth *Untimely Meditation (Richard Wagner in Bayreuth)* was the strongest expression of Nietzsche's change and showed his difficulty in publicly praising Wagner, although Nietzsche himself had in the meantime become critically detached from Wagner's art. As was always the case with Nietzsche, personal things had contributed to his change of attitude. His intimate contact with the Wagners could not go on in the old way after the composer moved to Bayreuth and the geographic distance between the friends increased. Nietzsche had gone to Bayreuth for the dedication of the *Festspielhaus* in May 1872; in late autumn he had met Richard and Cosima in Strassburg. But during Christmas vacation 1872/73, when Nietzsche was in Naumburg, he turned down an invitation from Wagner, which annoyed the composer greatly. Nietzsche, every bit as vulnerable as Wagner, was alarmed, and went to see him with Rohde at Eastertime. But now, Nietzsche was unable to restore the intimate atmosphere that had once prevailed in Switzerland. He had hoped to discuss his half-completed manuscript, *Philosophy in the Tragic Age of the Greeks;* instead, the conversation centered on Wagner's worries. The Bayreuth project was afflicted as much by lack of funds as lack of public interest. Nietzsche felt a childlike disappointment that the Master showed no inclination to talk about ancient Greek thought; and what was worse, he was disappointed at finding an entirely different Wagner. This one was not the exiled poet and musician, with whom he had shared intellectual pleasures, but a man engaged in active struggle for the realization of his life's work. Nietzsche was in a quandary. His uncertainty found expression in a letter to Wagner (April 18, 1873):

"Most honored Master, I think constantly about the days I spent in Bayreuth, and everything I learned and experienced in such a short time spreads out before me in greater and greater abundance. I can only too well understand your dissatisfaction with me during my stay, without being able to do anything about it, for I learn and perceive very slowly, and every moment I spend in your company I learn something

I have never thought of previously and wish to retain. I fully realize, dear Master, that such a visit can offer you little relaxation and must at times be unbearable. I often wished for at least the appearance of greater freedom and independence, but in vain. Enough! Please accept me as a pupil alone, possibly with a pen in my hand and a notebook before me. . . . I grow more melancholy every day when I really sense how much I would like somehow to help you, be of use to you, and how totally incapable I am to do this, so that I cannot even contribute to your diversion and amusement." [38]

This letter reads like the foolish reaction of a lover who can barely hide his jealousy. And yet Nietzsche's bondage to and dependence on Wagner are no longer as strong as they seem. A few weeks earlier, Nietzsche had written to Gersdorff that he was loyal to Wagner "in all important matters," but as for "minor and subordinate points and a certain necessary, almost 'salubrious' abstinence from frequent personal association," [39] he had to preserve his freedom. This is a clear indication of Nietzsche's irresolute attitude toward Wagner. His admiration for the Master conflicted with his own unwillingness to subordinate himself and with his tendency to play the dominant role in all personal relationships, and especially in friendships. Thus it may have been a feeling of competitiveness that opened Nietzsche's eyes, gradually making him see Wagner in a different light and view his work more critically, so that fanatical passion, changing imperceptibly at first and then relentlessly, became a love-hate attitude. It may also have been the love-hate feeling of the frustrated composer in Nietzsche— such imponderabilia could easily have played their part.

However, the friendship did not seem to be in serious danger. Nietzsche's letter to Wagner on the composer's sixtieth birthday in May 1873 was full of genuine warmth; and in the fall, Nietzsche had a chance to offer his friend true help. The *Festspielhaus* committee asked Nietzsche to author an appeal to the general public for financial contributions. Nietzsche drafted a rather unsuitable pamphlet called *Warning Cry to the Germans*, a peevish outburst against those who were indifferent to Wagner's art. Wagner gave his approval to the pamphlet; but the delegates of the Wagner clubs, who met in Bayreuth from October 30 to November 3, rejected it, substituting a milder appeal by another writer. Thus Nietzsche could not offer practical help in that manner to the jeopardized undertaking. However, in the summer of 1876, in time for the opening of the first Bayreuth festival, he publicly championed Wagner's cause once more by putting out the fourth *Untimely Meditation*.

RICHARD WAGNER IN BAYREUTH

Nietzsche had already written the first eight sections of the fourth *Meditation* in 1875, but in October the work came to a standstill. Only the fact that the festival was really taking place induced him to quickly complete the essay in the spring of 1876. *Richard Wagner in Bayreuth* does more to reveal the change in Nietzsche than to add anything new about Wagner. It presents a Nietzsche who, albeit convinced of the greatness of Wagner's art, shows restraint in his admiration. There is no enthusiastic exuberance; the phenomenon of Wagner is suddenly open to analysis; the man, the musician, and the writer Wagner are studied in succession. The first few parts of the treatise contain a psychologically accurate portrait of the composer, his significance, the difficulties he faced, and his daring struggle. Nietzsche depicts Wagner as a great personality, comparing him to classical antiquity and attacking reason, enlightenment, and the influence of thought as pernicious to life. The criticism of the contemporary perversion of civilization is followed in sections six and seven by several hymnic passages which seem like a return to *The Birth of Tragedy,* and celebrate Wagner as a dithyrambic dramatist. But Nietzsche already mentions the "mysterious opposition" into which anyone contemplating such a personality is driven. Whereas the work was begun under the impression that the Bayreuth idea was in jeopardy, the closing portions were written in a state of confidence concerning the festival scheduled for that summer. The change in conditions may have been a reason for the contradictions and lack of unity characterizing this *Meditation.* But an even more important factor was Nietzsche's loss of faith in Wagner. And the feeble apologetics toward the end of the essay do little to hide the criticism, e.g. when Nietzsche tells his readers:

"Above all, no one reflecting about Wagner as a poet and molder of language ought to forget that Wagner's dramas are not meant to be read and therefore should not be importuned with the demands made on spoken drama." [40]

Which is just another way of admitting that Wagner's language is inadequate. Wagner allegedly has something of Demosthenes about him: ". . . the terrible earnestness of the matter at hand and the powerful grip." [41] These words may sound like hero worship, but they are also critical; Wagner does not possess the relaxed cheerfulness which Nietzsche praised so highly in Schopenhauer. Wagner as a writer evinces the compulsion of the brave man whose right hand has been smashed and who continues to fence with his left hand. "He is a constant invalid when writing because a temporarily insuperable need deprives him of the right communication in his fashion, in the form of a shining and triumphant model." [42] Lastly, Nietzsche asks what Wagner's significance will be for Germany and finds the critical answer in the last sentence of the *Meditation:* ". . . something that he cannot be for all of us, not the prophet of the future, as perhaps he would like to be, but the interpreter and glorifier of the past." [43] This was Nietzsche's rupture with Wagner on the eve of the first Bayreuth festival: Wagner is no seer—Nietzsche wanted to claim the gift of prophecy for himself. And so his treatise, outwardly a *Festschrift* for Bayreuth, actually revealed that Nietzsche was breaking with many things, such as the idea, expressed in *The Birth of Tragedy,* that art can redeem life. The dithyrambic artist no longer takes precedence, art can never be more than a simplified picture of the complexities of life.

As a matter of fact, the last of the *Untimely Meditations* was written during a growing alienation from Wagner. In 1873, the first disappointments in the friendship had come about. In January, Wagner was annoyed that Nietzsche hadn't accepted his invitation; and in April, Nietzsche was depressed by his visit to Bayreuth. In the autumn, his pamphlet was rejected. In early summer of 1874, he turned down a particularly friendly invitation from the Wagners and went to an Alpine village to finish his essay on Schopenhauer. In August, however, Nietzsche and his sister did go to Bayreuth, to the great joy of Richard and Cosima Wagner. But Nietzsche was reticent and aloof, and seemed intent on baiting Wagner. He had heard Brahms in Basel on July 8 and 9, and acquired the piano version of the *Triumphlied.* Wagner felt a strong dislike for Brahms' music, and Nietzsche had brought the score along merely to irritate him. Wagner exploded: "I realized that Nietzsche was saying: look, here's someone else who can produce something worthwhile. Well, one evening I blew up, and how I blew up!" Two vain, vulnerable natures collided. But while Wagner's anger evaporated almost instantly, it took Nietzsche a long time to get over it. After this unfortunate visit, Nietzsche did not see Wagner for two years. It was only in July 1876, during the rehearsals for the festival, that Nietzsche returned to Bayreuth.

And yet Richard and Cosima did everything they could for their friend. They heaped enormous praise on his essay *Schopenhauer as Educator* and were deeply concerned about Nietzsche's welfare. Nietzsche never intended to end the *Untimely Meditations* with an encomium of Wagner. Instead, he began working on a manuscript entitled *We*

Philologists, a reformulation of older ideas on the Greeks and education. His interest soon flagged, and the essay was never completed. This,
too, may be taken as a sign of change, uncertainty, and crisis. In the
fall, he spent a great deal of time with a group of young colleagues
in Basel, which brought him some relaxation. But by the end of the
year, Nietzsche was so downhearted that Wagner wrote to him in un-
diminished and sincere friendship, begging him to change his mode of
life:

"Your letter has once again caused us great anxiety about you. My
wife will write to you in greater detail within the next few days. Today
is the second day of Christmas and I have a quarter of an hour at my
disposal that I would like to devote to you—at the risk of vexing you—
in order to let you know what we have been saying about you. Among
other things, I found that in all my life I've never had such masculine
company as the people you spend your evenings with in Basel; if all of
you are hypochondriacs then the whole thing isn't worth very much. . . .
I felt you ought to marry or compose an opera; one would be as good
or as harmful as the other. But I think marriage would be better.

"For the time being, I could recommend a palliative; but you always
arrange your medicine chest in such a way that no one else can add a
remedy. For example, we arranged our household, etc., in such a way
as to prepare accommodations for you, something that I was never
offered even in times of utmost hardship; you were to spend your whole
summer vacation here. But—with utmost caution you informed us in
early winter of your decision to spend the holidays on a lofty and
lonely Swiss mountain! Doesn't it sound like a careful defense against
any possible invitations on our part? We can be something for you
why do you so urgently scorn the idea?—Gersdorff and the whole
Basilium could consent to your coming here. . . .

"I don't want to talk about you anymore, because it's quite useless.

"For God's sake, marry a rich woman. Why does Gersdorff have to
be a man! Take a trip, add to your knowledge, experience all the marvelous things that make Hillebrand [the author of a theory of aesthetics
on which Wagner and Nietzsche disagreed] so well-rounded and (in
your eyes) enviable, and—compose your opera, it will undoubtedly
be abominably difficult to perform.—What Satan made you a
pedagogue!—" [44]

In January 1875, Cosima Wagner wrote to Nietzsche asking whether his
sister Elisabeth could take care of the Wagner children and household
in Bayreuth while they went on a trip. Nietzsche gave his immediate

consent; he welcomed the idea of doing something for his friends with-out any direct involvement on his own part. Still, during this time, there were moments of genuine enthusiasm for Wagner. At Easter 1875, Nietzsche bought the piano arrangement of *Götterdämmerung* and wrote: "This is heaven on earth." He also began his essay *Wagner in Bayreuth,* very intent on doing something for Wagner. In August of the same year, while taking the cure at Steinabad in the Black Forest, Nietzsche wrote to Rohde:

"And I'm not in Bayreuth! . . . I can hardly understand it. And yet in spirit I'm there more than three quarters of the day, and flit around Bayreuth like a ghost. You needn't be afraid of making my soul greedy, tell me a little too much, dear friend; when I'm out walking I conduct whole passages of the music I know by heart, and I hum along." But two months later, in another letter to Rohde: "My *Meditation* 'Richard W. in Bayreuth' will not be printed. It's almost done, but I've fallen far short of the demands I made on myself; and so its only value for me lies in its being a new orientation toward the most difficult point in our experiences. I'm not above it all, and I realize that my new orien-tation isn't completely successful—and that I certainly can't be of any help to others!" [45]

Nietzsche was quite conscious of his own failure in regard to Wagner as the most difficult point of his life. Nevertheless, the essay was, as we know, finished in the spring of 1876 and printed by July. Nietzsche sent two copies to Bayreuth, but he felt uneasy about it: "This time I find it impossible to guess your reaction to these confessions." [46] However, his fear was groundless: Wagner, overworked as he was, evidently failed to notice either the change in Nietzsche's attitude or the critical barbs. He replied: "My friend! Your book is colossal!—How did you man-age to understand me so well?—Come as soon as you can, attend the rehearsals and get used to the impressions." [47]

Nietzsche quickly took him up on it. Toward the last of July, he arrived in Bayreuth, but a few days later he complained to his sister: "I long to be somewhere else. . . . I'm sick of the whole thing." [48]

His aesthetic dissatisfaction was accompanied by a rapid deteriora-tion of his health. Just before the first dress rehearsal, Nietzsche fled into the Bavarian Forest. Here he jotted down notes for *Human, All-Too-Human,* and nothing exhibits more clearly how far he had withdrawn from the whole Wagner fanfare. After ten days, he returned, at his sister's entreaties, for the public premiere of *Rheingold.* Although he stayed on in Bayreuth, he attended no other performances of the *Ring.*

Mentally, Nietzsche's break with Wagner was complete. Twelve years later, in *Nietzsche vs. Wagner,* he was to render an account of the entire experience: "As early as summer 1876, in the middle of the first festival, I took leave of Wagner. I cannot bear ambivalence; ever since his return to Germany, he has lowered himself step by step to everything I despise—even anti-Semitism. . . . It was really high time that I took my leave: this was instantly proven to me. Richard Wagner, outwardly the conquering hero, in reality a rotting, despairing *décadent,* suddenly dropped, helpless and broken, before the Christian cross. . . ." [49]

The final meeting took place that autumn in Sorrento. Nietzsche spent the whole winter at the home of Malwida von Meysenbug; it was probably a coincidence that the Wagners spent their vacation in Sorrento from October 5 to November 5. During a walk on one of his last days there, Wagner talked about *Parsifal,* which he had just begun working on. Wagner spoke with the vitality and eloquence which Nietzsche had once so greatly admired. The composer revealed his earnest interest in the specifically Christian motifs of the Parsifal legend. Nietzsche lapsed into an icy silence, excused himself abruptly, and vanished into the dusk. The two men never met again.

Thus the most important friendship in Nietzsche's life came to an end. The personal aftermath, which made the tacit break official, did not occur until 1878. In January, Wagner, totally unaware of anything and without rancor toward Nietzsche, sent him a copy of *Parsifal.* Nietzsche said nothing to Wagner, but did not keep his criticism to himself when talking to friends. In May, *Human, All-Too-Human* having just been finished, he sent a copy of it with an inane dedication to Richard and Cosima Wagner. But Nietzsche's thinly disguised attacks against Wagner, who is addressed merely as *the Artist* in the book, understandably hurt the feelings of his Bayreuth friends. They maintained silence, and Wagner broke it only once; in the August issue of *Bayreuther Blätter* he published an article "The Audience and Popularity," which contained scornful criticism of Nietzsche's ideas. But otherwise Wagner, known for his maliciousness toward friends, controlled himself quite well. Nietzsche's sister tried to intercede in Bayreuth, but failed. The break was final.

4 ILLNESS

"I've reached the end of my thirty-fifth year; for 1500 years this was known as the 'midpoint of life.' Dante had his vision at that age and mentioned it in the first words of his Poem. Now, at the midpoint of my life, I am so surrounded by Death that he could seize hold of me at any moment. Considering the nature of my suffering, I am forced to picture a sudden convulsive death (although I would much prefer a slow, clearheaded death, that would allow me to still talk to my friends, even if it is more painful). Thus, I feel like the oldest of men; but also because I have done my life's work. A good drop of oil was poured out through me, I'm fully aware of it, and others will not let me forget it. Actually, I've made the test for my observations of life; many others still have that ahead of them. My mood has not yet been depressed by my sustained and painful suffering, at times I even seem to feel more cheerful and benevolent than ever before in my life. To whom do I owe this bracing and ameliorative effect? Not to any human being because, with very few exceptions, all of them have gotten 'annoyed at me' in these past few years and have made no bones about letting me know." [50]

FRIENDSHIP AND MARRIAGE PLANS

Nietzsche, who wrote these lines on September 11, 1878 from St. Moritz to his friend Peter Gast, was already in the worst of health during the period discussed in the foregoing chapter. His various physical ailments, which afflicted him almost constantly and grew more violent and malignant, were accompanied by a problem originating in his childhood: his "Leiden an der Welt"—suffering from the world—his difficulties in human relationships, his overdemanding attitude toward his friends. Not only Wagner was "annoyed" with Nietzsche. Ritschl, his teacher and fatherly friend, died in 1876; but his goodwill had vanished long before. And the friendship with Rohde, who was now a professor at Jena, had cooled. The break with Gersdorff came when the latter decided to marry an Italian girl and Nietzsche butted in, trying to dissuade him from going through with it. To be sure, new friends replaced the old ones: Malwida von Meysenbug, Paul Rée, and, most important of all, Heinrich Köselitz, known to Nietzsche scholars by his pseudonym Peter Gast.

Peter Gast, a young musician, had come to Basel in 1875 for the purpose of meeting Nietzsche. Highly impressed by Nietzsche's writings, Gast grew to admire the philosopher so much, after getting to know him personally and attending his lectures, that he became Nietzsche's utterly obedient follower. Nietzsche for his part took a liking to Gast as a musician and human being; and for practical reasons, the new friend was soon indispensable. Peter Gast's penmanship was beautiful and extremely easy to read. Nietzsche could dictate to him, and Gast would prepare the clean copy for the printer, thereby being of great help to Nietzsche and gaining his full confidence.

A year later—after Bayreuth—Nietzsche became friends with Richard von Seydlitz, a painter and writer. Since his illness was growing worse, Nietzsche needed not only a self-sacrificing friend like Gast, but constant attendance as well. This was probably the only reason why Nietzsche let his sister enter so deeply into his life and take over more and more of his affairs. As of August 1875, Elisabeth shared an apartment with her brother in Basel. But since she also had to take care of her mother in Naumburg, her help and attendance were sporadic, although Nietzsche called upon her services more and more. And so he continued his restless life, traveling from Basel to points all over Germany, Italy, and Switzerland, visiting friends, taking the cure at various baths, seeking to escape increasingly unbearable pain through a continual change of climate. Nietzsche was endlessly in search of a physically and psychologically wholesome environment.

In 1876 and 1877, he tried a different solution, which Wagner had recommended in early 1875. Nietzsche considered the possibility of marriage in order to find some peace of mind in his restless existence.

He spent March and April 1876 on Lake Geneva—it was one of his countless rest cures. Gersdorff accompanied him, and the two friends read Manzoni's *I promessi sposi* together. During this month, Nietzsche made the acquaintance of Mathilde Trampedach, a young Dutch girl; several days later, after a four-hour promenade, he asked for her hand. A written proposal was made on the eve of his departure. Nietzsche, undoubtedly inhibited about taking such steps, was encouraged by the fact that Fräulein Trampedach was reading Longfellow's *Excelsior*, in which she had found a *Lebensanschauung*, a view of life. So Nietzsche resolved to write her the letter, which, although courteously worded, sounds awkward and rude:

"GENEVA, APRIL 11, 1876

"*Mein Fräulein! Tonight you will write something for me, I will write something for you.*

"*Gather all the courage in your heart so as not to take fright at the question I now put to you: Will you marry me? I love you, and I feel as if you already belonged to me. Not a word about the sudden-ness of my love. At least there is no fault in that, and therefore there is nothing to apologize for. But I would like to know whether you feel as I do—that we were no strangers to one another, not even for an instant! Don't you also think that by marrying, each of us would be-come freer and better than we could be if we remained single, that is, excelsior? Would you take a chance to go with me, with someone sincerely striving to be free and better? On all paths of life and thought? Now be candid and don't hold anything back. No one knows about this letter and my question except for our mutual friend Herr von Senger. Tomorrow, at 11 a.m., I am taking the express back to Basel, I have to; you will find my Basel address enclosed. If you can say 'yes!' to my question, I will ask you for your mother's address and write to her immediately. If you can manage to make up your mind quickly, with yes! or no—then a note from you can reach me until 10 o'clock tomorrow at the Hôtel Garni de la Poste.*

"*Good luck and best wishes for all time from your*

"*Friedrich Nietzsche.*" [51]

This was an abrupt but spiritless courtship revealing little of Nietz-sche's actual feelings and demonstrating his inhibitions all the more clearly: the lover announces his departure and asks for a written reply. It was only later, after getting to know Lou Salomé, that he once more thought of marrying. In Sorrento, however, it was Malwida von Meysen-

Bayreuth: Festival House.

Richard Wagner.

Cosima Wagner,
marble bust by G. Kietz.

Elisabeth Nietzsche.

bug who suggested the idea of marriage. Thus, on April 25, 1877, he wrote to his sister:

"Nothing more cheerful than your letter, dear sister, which hit the nail on the head in all points. I was in such a bad state! Within the space of two weeks, I spent six days in bed after six major attacks, the last one positively maddening. I got back on my feet, and Fräulein von Meysenbug was laid low with rheumatism for three days. In the depths of our misery we had a good laugh when I read her a few choice passages of your letter.—Miss von Meysenbug has a plan which is to be steadfastly pursued, and you are to help us carry it out. We have convinced ourselves that my university existence cannot continue, that I can go on with it only by sacrificing all my more important projects and in addition totally ruining my health. Naturally, I shall still have to spend next winter there, but by Easter 1878 it will be over, if the other tactics work—to wit, a marriage with a woman who will be right for me but of necessity wealthy. 'Good, but rich,' as Miss M. said, and we laughed about the 'but.' With her, I would then spend the next few years in Rome, which is equally good for health, society, and my studies. The plan is to be set in motion this summer, in Switzerland, so that I would return to Basel as a married man. Various 'beings' have been invited to Switzerland, some of whom you've never heard of, for instance Elise Bülow from Berlin, Elsbeth Brandes from Hanover. As far as intellectual qualities go, I still think Nat. Herzen is the most suitable. You helped quite a bit with my idealization of little Miss Köckert in Geneva! All due praise for that! But still, it's a doubtful matter; and as for money?—" [52]

That was how matters stood at this point. The fact that Nietzsche was moved to a pure marriage of convenience for entirely bourgeois motives does not fit in with the image of the loner, but it does give us some idea of the extent of his physical suffering. Yet in June of the same year he already thought: "Marriage, though highly desirable—is most improbable, I know for certain!"

NIETZSCHE GIVES UP HIS PROFESSORSHIP

Sickness and pain became incessant. Nietzsche had to take more and more leaves of absence from his teaching job. And since his marital plans failed to materialize, there was only one other possibility, which he had already indicated, namely to resign from the university. Moreover, in the summer of 1878, outward circumstances made Nietzsche's life increasingly difficult; in late June, the menage in Basel was dissolved, because his sister settled down permanently with their mother in Naumburg. In early 1879, his health declined further; chronic attacks accompanied by violent headaches and pains in the eyes as well as constant vomiting became habitual. Nietzsche was thus forced to submit his resignation to the president of the canton of Basel on May 2. Six weeks later, his retirement was pronounced officially, and the university released him from his contract with genuine regret. Despite all difficulties, Nietzsche's work and accomplishments were held in high esteem. He was granted a yearly pension of 3000 Swiss francs. His last two lecture courses, in the winter semester of 1878/79, dealt with *Greek Lyric Poets* and *An Introduction to the Study of Plato*. First, Nietzsche and his sister went to Bremgarten Castle near Bern; then, shortly thereafter, when Elisabeth had to return to her mother, Overbeck's mother-in-law in Zurich began to look after Nietzsche. In late June, Nietzsche visited the Upper Engadine for the first time, and here he immediately found some relief.

". . . Perhaps St. Moritz is the right place after all. I feel as if I were in the Promised Land. . . . For the first time, I feel true relief. . . . It's so soothing. I want to stay here for a long time." And two weeks later: "I'm often sick, I've been in bed four days already, and every day brings its suffering, and yet! I can endure it here more than anywhere else. It's as if I had been seeking something for a long time and finally found it. I no longer believe I'll get better, much less recover. But being able to bear it is a great deal." [53]

CASE HISTORY

For several decades now, Nietzsche's illness has been giving rise to numerous studies, often with sharply divergent conclusions. In his Nietzsche biography, Karl Jaspers, carefully summarizing the major facts and the prevailing diagnoses, shows how much has to be left open. The universally accepted thesis is that Nietzsche's mental breakdown, which became quite manifest toward the close of 1888, was in all probability a symptom of paralysis. This in turn has often led to the assumption that the whole history of Nietzsche's illness may be understood from this point of view and that all the physical troubles of the preceding years are to be regarded as the preliminary stages of paralysis. The origin of the disease would then have to date from Nietzsche's university days, when the young student may have been exposed to a syphilitic infection. In his *Memories of Nietzsche*, Deussen recalls that while his friend was visiting Cologne, a porter took him to a brothel supposedly by mistake. According to Deussen, Nietzsche told his friend about the incident the next day, melodramatically recounting his escape from the ladies of easy virtue. Even if the account is reliable, it is still questionable whether an infection took place, or if it did, that it caused the brain disease.

♦ There is a controversial theory that Nietzsche himself brought on his illness through a misuse of toxicants and medicines. Others believe that the symptoms appearing as of 1873 were linked with a psychoneurotic process touched off by the mental estrangement from Richard Wagner. Speculations of this sort tend to be of little use, even becoming absurd when the claim is made that after 1866 Nietzsche's total output was the product of a deranged mind. There was certainly a relation between sickness and work in Nietzsche's life, but the problem remains "mysterious," because we know too little about what caused his malady. However, we must not forget that specific symptoms of Nietzsche's ailment occurred as early as his boyhood. In the summer of 1856, while attending the cathedral *Gymnasium*, he had been granted a leave of absence because of constant headaches and pains in his eyes. In 1862, at Pforta, the violent headaches returned. A medical report at Pforta describes Nietzsche as "solid and thickset, with conspicuously glassy eyes, shortsighted, and frequently troubled by metastatic headaches." During the 1870s the pains increased, turning into migrainoid attacks. They probably had no connection with the chest injury resulting from Nietzsche's riding accident during his basic training (March 1868) or the dysentery and throat diphtheria he caught during the war (1870). The dysentery was no doubt partially responsible for the abdominal disorders afflicting Nietzsche for many years after. In 1879, Nietzsche's general state of health declined so rapidly that by the end of the year it seems to have reached a nadir. At times, an attack even led to loss of consciousness. Whether Nietzsche really believed early in 1880 that the end was near remains an open question, since Karl Schlechta has proved that the letters of farewell dated 12/31/1879 and 1/16/1881 were subsequent forgeries by his sister. It is a fact that during the 1880s Nietzsche's attacks diminished greatly, that he suddenly experienced euphoric moods such as he had never known, creative periods of utmost rapture which were followed by periods of emptiness and uneasiness. Jaspers has pointed out that the symptoms which Nietzsche himself describes as appearing in this later phase of his productivity are far different from those of the 1870s. Moreover, prior to the 80s, Nietzsche cannot be called mentally ill. On the other hand, we can perfectly well understand that if a man has been afflicted by various ailments since his earliest youth, certain reactions and habits may be influenced by his ill health. Some scholars have claimed that Nietzsche's break with Wagner precipitated neurotic disorders. Yet the opposite could just as easily be true, i.e. that Nietzsche's catastrophic state of health contributed to the break by causing the hypersensitive and irritable philosopher to overreact.

HUMAN, ALL-TOO-HUMAN

During the relentless decline of his health, Nietzsche wrote *Human, All-Too-Human*. The sketches, begun in 1876 during his escape from Bayreuth, appeared in 1878. They were followed by supplements: *Mixed Opinions and Maxims* (1879) and *The Wanderer and His Shadow* (1850), both of which Nietzsche reprinted in a single volume (1886), calling it Volume II of *Human, All-Too-Human*. The very size of this work (nearly 600 pages in the Schlechta edition) proves that despite his illness and vagrant life, Nietzsche wrote almost constantly during those years.

Whether in Basel or in Bad Ragaz, in Naumburg or Bad Bex (Canton Waadt), in Chur, in Riva (on Lake Garda), or in Venice, which he first visited in the spring of 1880 with Peter Gast and never stopped loving thereafter—wherever Nietzsche went, he must have been working on his manuscripts incessantly, adjusting his work methods to his wanderings. Because of his illnesses and his never-ending travels, he could not manage continuous work at a desk. Instead, there was a prolific output of brief sketches, memoranda, aphorisms, and fragmentary essays, which soon grew into an extensive mass. Nietzsche could select any of the material at an appropriate time, revise it, and polish it up into a final version.

The numerous voyages were not without their hardships, difficulties, and irritations. In a letter to Malwida von Meysenbug (Lugano, May 13, 1877), Nietzsche described his trip from Sorrento back to Switzerland. The graphic account leaves nothing to the imagination:

"The human misery brought on by a sea voyage is terrible and yet ridiculous, which is what I occasionally feel about my headaches, that can come on even when the rest of my body is glowing with health—in short, today I'm back again in the mood of a 'cheerful cripple,' whereas on the boat I had only the blackest thoughts, and as for suicide, I was only uncertain about where the sea was deepest, so that I wouldn't be fished back out again and in addition would have to pay my rescuers a fearful amount of money to show my gratitude. Moreover, I experienced the worst state of seasickness when violent stomach pains joined forces with my headache to torture me; it was a 'memory of fading times.' To make matters worse, I had to change my position three to eight times a minute by day and night; to have the smells and conversations of a feasting crowd in closest proximity at such a time is outrageously disgusting. In the harbor at Livorno, it was a rainy night; all the same, I wanted to get out, but cold-blooded promises of the captain kept me back. Everything and everyone in the ship was romping about noisily, the pots were jumping and came to life, the children were bawling, the tempest howling; 'eternal sleeplessness was my lot,' a poet would say. The disembarkation brought new suffering; filled with my awful headache, I wore powerful spectacles on my nose for hours and distrusted everybody. The customs people were tolerable, but the most important thing of all slipped my mind; I forgot to register my baggage for the railroad. Off I rode to the marvelous Hotel National, with two rascals on the coach box who tried with all their might to drop me at a miserable trattoria; my baggage kept changing hands constantly; some man or other was always panting along in front of me with my trunk. A couple of times I flew into a rage, intimidating the coachman; his crony took off. Do you know how I got into the Hotel de Londres? I don't know, but it was fine. Only my entrance was ghastly, because a whole crowd of rowdies wanted to be paid off. I went to bed immediately, feeling very ill! On Friday, a gloomy, rainy day, I pulled myself together around noon and went to the gallery at the Palazzo Brignole; and amazingly enough, it was the sight of these family portraits that buoyed me up and aroused my enthusiasm; a Brignole on horseback, and the whole pride of the family in the eye of this powerful steed— that was something for my depressed humanity! Personally I hold Van Dyck and Rubens in higher esteem than all the other painters in the world. The remaining pictures left me cold, with the exception of a dying Cleopatra by Guercino. I came to life again and spent the rest of the day peacefully and courageously in my hotel. The next morning brought a different amusement. I had made the trip from Genoa to Milan with a very agreeable young ballerina of a theater in Milan: Camilla *era molto simpatica.* Oh! you should have heard my Italian. Were I a pasha, I would have taken her along to Pfäfers, where, renouncing all intellectual pursuits, I would have had her dance for me. Every so often, I still get annoyed at myself for not having spent at least a few days in Milan on her account. Now I was nearly in Switzerland, and I rode along the first stretch of the Saint Gotthard railway, which was just completed, from Como to Lugano. How did I ever come to Lugano? I didn't really want to, but here I am. As I crossed the Swiss border in a violent rainstorm, there came an unusually strong flash of lightning and peal of thunder. I took it as a good omen, and I won't deny that the closer I drew to the mountains the better I felt. In Chiasso, my baggage rode off on two separate trains, there was hopeless confusion, and then on top of it all the customs. Even my two umbrellas followed contrary instincts. A good porter came to my aid, he spoke the first Swiss German that I heard. You can imagine that I was rather moved at the sound of it; I suddenly realized that I prefer living with Swiss Germans rather than Germans." [54]

What adventures and what torments! A sophisticated traveler, Nietzsche always managed to cope with all such difficulties, and even took pleasure in writing down all the delightful and amusing things that happened to him in the course of his travels. But the hardships that the invalid was exposed to do give proof of the unusual encumbrances on Nietzsche's productivity. This was the atmosphere in which he brought forth Human, All-Too-Human.

Nietzsche subtitled his treatise A Book for Free Spirits, and it can actually be understood as a unique, great attempt on his part to find himself and burst the fetters of traditional ideas which tortured him. He succeeded in two ways: Nietzsche the philosopher discovered a new understanding of life, and Nietzsche the writer had found a suitable mode of expression—a predominantly aphoristic style. It is unnecessary to add that the work is autobiographical in many respects. But we can point to several people whose influence is manifest. First of all, there was Nietzsche's new friend Paul Rée, who had published his Psychological Meditations in 1875. Rée stressed—with no great originality—the importance of self-love for human behavior. Nietzsche was deeply impressed. But the other influences were the French moralists and writers of epigrams: Montaigne, La Rochefoucauld, La Bruyère, Chamfort, and Stendhal. It was here that Nietzsche found the models for his finely polished style, for the aphoristic wording of his thoughts, a sarcastically and skeptically objective approach to any commitment. All his previous writings were like preludes; this book initiated the work of Nietzsche's maturity. A book for free spirits! For men who are free of superstition and idealism. First of all, as far as Nietzsche was concerned, this meant liberating himself from Schopenhauer and the fallacies of metaphysics, as he once had from the Christian dogma; freeing himself, too, from the aesthetic views he owed to Wagner. Nietzsche set himself up as an example of a free spirit, and this is revealed more than once in the essay: e.g. "I am passionately fond of independence, to which I sacrifice everything—probably because I have the most dependent of souls, and the tiniest cords torment me more than chains do other people." [55]

There is something new here. Under the influence of Schopenhauer's ethics and Kant's epistemology, Nietzsche had always professed that the world is not as it appears to us, that phenomena and our ideas are false; yet he did believe that reality per se has a deeper meaning. Now, however, he saw that reality has no meaning of its own. It exists and has a being, but is devoid of any inherent meaning. "Perhaps we know . . . that the *ding an sich* deserves Homeric laughter; it appeared to be so much, nay, everything; but actually it is empty, that is, empty of meaning!" [56] Yet there is no metaphysical world either, no "actual" reality beyond things, i.e. beyond superficial phenomena, no law-giving cosmic Disposer and no afterlife. Ergo, the traditional ethical categories are meaningless; good and evil do not exist in themselves. So-called evil deeds are motivated by self-preservation, good is based on conventions:

"All 'evil' deeds are motivated by the instinct of self-preservation or, more precisely, by the individual's desire for pleasure and the avoidance of pain; such motivation is not evil. 'Causing pain as such' does not exist, except in the minds of philosophers, nor does 'causing pleasure as such' exist (sympathy or pity in Schopenhauer's sense of the word). Morality is preceded by constraint or pressure. For a while it *is* a constraint to which one gives in to avoid pain. Later it becomes a custom, then free obedience, and finally almost an instinct. At this point, like all ingrained or innate habits, it is linked with pleasure—and is dubbed virtue." [57]

Even art has lost its dominant role. In part IV, *From the Souls of Artists and Writers*, Nietzsche revises his own Dionysian idea that art can redeem life. He bids farewell to Wagner, who, referred to only as "the Artist," actually belongs to the "Twilight of Art":

"The artist will soon be viewed as a splendid vestige and, like a marvelous stranger on whose strength and beauty the fortune of earlier times depended, he will be paid such honors as we do not instantly grant to our own kind. The best thing about us may be a legacy of the feelings of earlier times, which we can no longer reach directly; the sun has already set, but the heaven of our life is still resplendent with its rays, although we no longer see it." [58]

Another new feature is evident. The anti-Enlightenment philosopher Nietzsche discloses an inclination toward skeptical rationality. The collapse of Dionysian irrationalism, the denial of metaphysical transcendence is followed by an appeal to the "freedom of reason." "Man by himself" can escape the desert of reality only as a wanderer constantly regaining detached distance; only this aimless wandering guarantees an openness to the world and thereby freedom. In #638 (which closes Volume I), Nietzsche's description of this state is incomparable, and the beauty of his language anticipates *Thus Spake Zarathustra:*

"The wanderer.—He who to any degree whatsoever has reached the freedom of reason can only feel like a wanderer on the earth—albeit not as a traveler to an ultimate destination; for there is no such thing. He will observe and keep his eyes open to everything that happens in the world; for this reason, he must not attach his heart too firmly to any single thing; he must have within himself something of the wandering, which takes pleasure in change and ephemeralness. Naturally, such a man will have bad nights, when he is tired, and the gates of the town that was to offer him repose are shut; and perhaps, as in the Orient, the desert will reach as far as the gates, the beasts of prey will be howling, sometimes farther away, sometimes closer, a powerful wind will arise, thieves will take his draft animals. The terrible night will then descend like a second desert upon the desert, and his heart will be weary of wandering. And when the morning sun appears, ardent as a god of wrath, the city shall open, and in the faces of the inhabitants he will perhaps see more desert, filth, falsehood, and uncertainty than before the gates—and the day will be almost worse than the night. This may befall the wanderer; but then, to make up for it, there will come the blissful mornings of other places and days, when he shall see in the gray dawn the hosts of muses dancing by close to him in the mountain fog; and afterwards, in the harmony of the morning soul, he shall walk quietly beneath trees whose tops and foliage throw off only good and bright things, the gifts of all the free spirits who are at home in mountain forest and solitude, and who, in their sometimes gay, sometimes reflective fashion are wanderers and philosophers like him. Born out of the mysteries of dawn, they wonder how the day can have such a pure, radiant, transfigured, cheerful countenance between the hours of ten and twelve.—They are seeking the philosophy of morning." [59]

The twilight of art is followed by the dawn of philosophy, whose task it is to reverse all present values.

The addenda, *Mixed Opinions and Maxims* and *The Wanderer and His Shadow,* forming the second volume, are even more unsystematic variations on the new themes. But they often gain in concretion and

aphoristic terseness, for instance the thoughts on the future of Christianity, and especially the innumerable comments on the Germans,
German mentality, German traits and vices. Next to Heinrich Heine,
Nietzsche thus became the most perceptive critic of the Germans in the
nineteenth century. A great deal of what he says is still fresh, his
prophetic power is impressive, and his writings are as valid as ever.
An excellent example is Aphorism #324 in *Mixed Opinions:*

"A foreign traveler in Germany made statements eliciting like or dislike, depending on the area in which he chanced to be. All Swabians
who possess intellect—he would say—are coquettish.—The other Swabians, however, still think that Uhland was a poet and that Goethe was
immoral.—The best thing about the German novels that are acquiring
renown today is that you don't have to read them; you know them already.—The Berliner appears to be better-natured than the South German, because he is far too sarcastic and therefore can take sarcasm
himself; which is more than you can say for the South German.—The
intellect of the Germans is held down by their beer and their newspapers; it would be advisable for them to try tea and pamphlets, as
therapy of course.—. . . The most dangerous parts of Germany are
Saxony and Thuringia; nowhere else will you find more intellectual
activity and knowledge of human nature, as well as free-thinking, and
all of it is so discreetly hidden by the ugly dialect and the ardent officious-
ness of the inhabitants that you hardly realize that these are the intellectual bullies of Germany, and its teachers for good or evil.—The arrogance of the North German is held in check by his passion for obeying,
that of the South German is restrained by his love of comfort.—The
traveler voiced the opinion that German men had spouses who were
awkward, but thoroughly self-assured housewives; they spoke so persis-
tently well of themselves that they had almost convinced the world, and
in any event their husbands, of their peculiarly German housewife-
quality.—Whenever the conversation turned to German foreign and
domestic politics, he would say—he called it 'divulge'—that Germany's
greatest statesman did not believe in great statesmen.—He felt that
the future of the Germans was endangered and dangerous; for they had
forgotten how to enjoy themselves (something the Italians know so
well); instead, through the great gamble of wars and dynastic revolu-
tions they got so accustomed to emotion that consequently they would
some day have an émeute [riot]. For this is the strongest emotion that
a nation can give itself.—The German socialist is the most dangerous,
because he is not driven by any definite necessity; his suffering is not

knowing what he wants; thus, even if he achieves a great deal, he will still die in pleasure from desire, just like Faust, although presumably a very plebeian Faust. 'The Faust-demon,' cried the traveler in the end. 'by whom educated Germans were so terribly plagued, was exorcised by Bismarck; now, however, the devil has gotten hold of the pigs and is worse than ever before.' " [60]

His new work did not bring Nietzsche any new friends. We have already seen that *Human, All-Too-Human* confirmed the break with Wagner, but Rohde, too, was dissatisfied with the book which revealed a Nietzsche he could neither understand nor accept. He was particularly incensed at Nietzsche's denial that man is responsible for his own behavior in a basically senseless world: "No one can ever make me believe such a doctrine; no one does believe in it, not even you."

Nietzsche was well aware of the change within himself. And although his illness was almost more than he could bear, he viewed this book as the first step toward recovery, a process he described meticulously in a later foreword (1886). The privilege of the free spirit to live a life of endeavor and the will to health are stressed as much as the really new things that the desert wanderer encounters: ". . . the question mark of an increasingly dangerous curiosity. Can we not reverse all values? And might Good be Evil? And God merely an invention and subtlety of the devil? Is it possible that everything is ultimately false? And if we are the victims of deception, doesn't precisely this make us deceivers? Must we not be deceivers too?" [61] With these questions, Nietzsche seemed to be indicating the compass that was to denote his direction in wanderings filled with discovery. *Dawn. Thoughts about Moral Prejudices* is a direct continuation of the aphorisms in *Human, All-Too-Human*. The delicacies of his new stylistic freedom were savored fully, the theme was refined and treated in a lighter, more cheerful fashion, without revealing any really new insights. *The Gay Science,* a third book of aphorisms, is also part of this group of works based on the same material, the multitude of notes and sketches of past years. Although individually brilliant, they are marred in toto by a certain thematic monotony which makes whole sections of them seem almost interchangeable. At the same time, *The Gay Science* becomes a prelude to *Thus Spake Zarathustra*. Nietzsche saw himself as a convalescent.

5 TO THE LAND OF ZARATHUSTRA

In the spring of 1880, after a trip to Naumburg, Nietzsche went to Venice for the first time, accompanied by Peter Gast. With his health gradually improving, he read Stifter's *Nachsommer (Indian Summer)* and despite the nadir he had reached by the end of the year, he slowly began to work again. When the June heat became too much for him, he moved on to Marienbad in the Engadine, visited his mother and his sister in Naumburg that September, decided to go back south, met Overbeck in Basel, spent October on Lago Maggiore, and settled down in Genoa for the winter. As much as he loved the solitude in his Genoese garret, he spent a miserable southern winter without a stove and plagued by constant headaches. But all the same, he managed to finish the manuscript of *Dawn* by January 1881. Together with Gast, he passed the spring in a tiny mountain spa, Recoaro near Vicenza. It was only in summer, when he returned to the Engadine, that his condition improved perceptibly. By chance, he discovered the village of Sils-Maria in the Inn valley—the most beautiful part of one of the most beautiful valleys in the world. Entranced by the southern light that broke on the awe-inspiring gravity of the mountains, Nietzsche wrote to Peter Gast:

"On the other hand, I consider it my reward that this year revealed two things which belong to me and are very close to me: your music and this landscape. This isn't Switzerland or Recoaro, this is something entirely different, or at least something far more southern—I would have to go to the high plateaus on the Pacific coast of Mexico to find any-thing similar (e.g. Oaxaca) and they would have tropical vegetation. As things now stand, I want to try and keep this Sils-Maria." [62]

Overcome by a new feeling of elation, he sent home reassuring news about his health: "The word 'depressed' has never been less applicable to anyone. . . . I look marvelous; because of constant marching my muscles are almost like those of a soldier, stomach and abdomen are in good condition. And my nerves, considering the enormous demands made upon them, are splendid. . . ." [63]

This was slightly exaggerated, because only a few days later, in a letter to Overbeck, Nietzsche complained that his health was not what he had hoped for: "Exceptional weather here, too! Eternal changing of atmospheric conditions!—that will drive me out of Europe yet! I have to have a *clear* sky for *months* at a time, or I'll remain stagnant. Already six serious attacks, lasting two to three days!!" [64]

Nietzsche was always a demon for letter-writing. In those years he even used a typewriter for his correspondence, his penmanship being rather poor because his ocular disorders forced him to hold his head very close to the paper. But even the typewriter was often a nuisance. Thus, at the close of a letter to Paul Rée (March 21, 1882), he tells of his struggle with the insidious whims of the machine: "The typewriter refuses to go on, this is the spot where the ribbon was mended!" [65]

Yet his happiness in Sils was such as he had never known. He dis-covered Spinoza, and during that first summer there had a greatly inspiring idea—the eternal recurrence of the same, the key to *Zara-thustra*. We do not know what precipitated Nietzsche's euphoria (his first). We do not know whether he really recovered or the nature of his illness altered, whether an internal intellectual process of maturity reached a certain stage or whether it was the magic effect of Sils that wrought changes. In any case, Nietzsche had little desire to see any friends at this time; he even discouraged Paul Rée from visiting him. A recluse in a small house removed from the main road, he lived in a shady back room, which faced the woods and let in none of the bright light that his eyes could not endure.

Here he led the peaceful life of a philosopher: wandering along the lake and in the mountain forest, musing, busily reading and writing—and always secluded. This is the well-known image that has come down to us, the image of a lonesome Nietzsche. But these conditions are not conducive to the conception of a logical and systematic structure; they are part of a mood; vague feelings, desires, and the problems of the

Nietzsche house in Sils-Maria.

Nietzsche's typewriter.

,,*Carmen*''

MEINE LIEBEN KOENNTE ICH NUR AUCH SO VIEL
HEITERES MELDEN WIE VON EUCH KOMMT.ABER ICH
BIN IMMER WIE HALBTODT UND DER LETZTE ANFALL
GEHOERTE ZU MEINEN SCHLIMMSTEN.IN ALLEN ZWI
SCHENPAUSEN WIE ZWISCHEN ALLEM ELENDE SELBER
LACHEN WIR VIEL UND REDEN GUTE UND BOESE DI
NGE.VIELLEICHT BEGLEITE ICH DEN FREUND AUF
EINEM AUSFLUGE AN DIE RIVIERA.MOEGE SIE IHM
SO GEFALLEN ALS IHM GENUA GEFAELLT:ICH BIN
HIER DOCH SEHR ZU HAUSE.EINE MARQUESA
DORIA HAT MICH ANFRAGEN LASSEN OB ICH IHR
DEUTSCHEN UNTERRICHT GEBEN WOLLE=ICH HABE
NEIN GESAGT.DIE SCHREIBMASCHINE ·IST ZUNAECHST
ANGREIFENDER ALS IRGEND WELCHES SCHREIBEN.
WAEHREND DES GROSSEN CARNEVALZUGES WAREN
WIR AUF DEM FRIEDHOFE DEM SCHOENSTEN DER
SCHOENSTEN DER ERDE.MITTE MAERZ GEHT   REE
ZU FRL.VON MEYSENBUG NACH ROM.WIR BEIDE ZIE-
HEN GENUA DER SORRENTINISCHEN LANDSCHAFT
VOR.DREIMAL HABEN WIR IM MEERE GEBADET.
MIT DEM HERZLICHSTEN DANKE UND GRUSSE
        EUER   F.

Typewritten letter to Nietzsche's mother and his sister, March 1882.

Lou Salomé.

14.

Es könnte einmal eine
Zeit kommen, in welcher
man noch kleine philosophische
Denker große philosophische
Gedanken haben könnten.
*in welcher der "große Gedanke" einen Jemand davor abgiebt,
daß sein Urheber ein kleiner Denker ist.*

15.

Vielleicht würde der
ästlichste Philosoph nicht bis
zur Philosophie kommen,
*Der ... Philosoph würde vielleicht nicht bis
zum System kommen dürfen*

16.

Was den Denker über
die Dinge stellt, ist nicht
so sehr seine Geisteskraft
als seine Geistesrichtung (Nietzsche)

Aphorisms by Lou Salomé, with corrections by Nietzsche.

past. home and Christianity, friends and acquaintances, classical literature and Wagnerian music, malaise with the world and physical disorders. From this mood came the vision of the eternal recurrence as
something entirely new: "Thoughts have emerged on my horizon such
as I have never seen before.—. . . I guess I'll have to live a few years
more."

Despite great moodiness, his elation seemed to persist when he began
working on *The Gay Science* that winter. To his great delight, he heard
Bizet's *Carmen* for the first time in November; and he gave Book IV
of *The Gay Science*, at the end of which the figure of Zarathustra is
introduced, a surprisingly positive beginning on New Year's 1882:

"I want to learn more and more to see the necessary in things as
beauty—thus I will be one of those who make things beautiful. Amor
fati: from now on this will be my love! I will not wage war against ugli-
ness. I will not denounce nor will I even denounce the denouncers. Looking away will be my sole denial. And all in all, at some point I want to
become affirmative about everything!" [66]

Thus he had turned to a new philosophy that was affirmative of life
and yet anything but shallow optimism. The year in which he voiced
this programmatic desire brought him one of the strangest adventures
of his life.

LOU SALOMÉ

Toward the end of March 1882, Nietzsche was in Genoa. On a sudden
whim, he sailed for Messina, arriving with a bad case of seasickness.
Thrilled by the beautiful landscape and the Sicilian climate, he would
have preferred to remain there longer, but in April the sirocco drove
him away. And so, at Rée's and Malwida von Meysenbug's invitation,
he went to Rome. His friends brought him a new pupil: Lou Salomé.
The young Russian girl was unquestionably attractive (although not in
the usual sense) as well as extremely intelligent. Nietzsche fell in love
with her, and so did Paul Rée. And this time—as opposed to the superficial relationship several years earlier—Nietzsche was truly involved.
Lou in turn was drawn to and fascinated by him. Later on, she bril-
liantly described the impression he made on her:

"Loneliness—that was the first, strong impression created by Nietzsche's fascinating appearance. The casual observer may not have been
struck by anything unusual; a man of medium height, whose manner
of dress was exceedingly simple and yet exceedingly meticulous, with

calm features and brown hair combed straight back, he could be easily overlooked. The fine, highly expressive lines of the mouth were almost completely covered by a large mustache combed out toward the front; his laugh was quiet, he had a noiseless way of speaking, and walked in a cautious, pensive way, hunching his shoulders slightly; it was hard to imagine this figure in the middle of a crowd—he bore the stamp of one who stands apart, alone. Nietzsche's hands were so incomparably beautiful and nobly shaped that one could not help looking at them, and he himself believed that they revealed his spirit. . . . He ascribed a similar significance to his unusually small and finely modeled ears, claiming that they were true 'ears for things unheard.'

"His eyes spoke revealingly, too. Though purblind, they had nothing of the myopic's peering, unconsciously obtrusive blinking about them; they looked more like guardians and keepers of their own treasures, mute mysteries, which no impertinent eyes must touch. . . . Whenever he showed himself as he was, under the spell of a stimulating conversation with someone else, a poignant brilliance might light up and fade in his eyes;—but when his mood was somber, then loneliness would appear in them, dark and almost menacing, as if emerging from terrible depths.

"Nietzsche's behavior created a similar impression of reticence and secrecy. In everyday life he showed utmost courtesy and almost feminine gentleness, a constant, considerate equanimity—he derived great pleasure from and liked to practice elegant manners. But there was always a love of masquerade about it—a cloak and mask for his inner feelings, which were hardly ever laid bare. I remember that upon speaking with Nietzsche for the first time—it was at St. Peter's Church in Rome on a spring day—I was struck and misled during the first few minutes by his studied politeness. But the deception was short-lived, this lonely man wore his mask as awkwardly as someone from a desert or a mountain wears the coat of everyday people." [67]

Nietzsche was totally entranced by his new friendship, which came at a fortunate moment, for he had just completed the final draft of *The Gay Science*. Although he may have started thinking about *Zarathustra*, he was planning to give up writing for a longer period of time, and perhaps even to begin methodical studies again. His days in Rome passed quickly, and in May he, Lou, Lou's mother, and Rée went to Lucerne, a place filled with many memories for him. Nietzsche even took Lou to Tribschen and spoke enthusiastically about the happy times he had spent in Wagner's home; he told her about his youth and revealed to his understanding pupil his innermost, still developing philosophical thoughts. He felt he had met someone who inspired him with the hope that his shattered life might be made whole again. No doubt about it—Nietzsche, the lonely wanderer, had fallen in love and made all the plans that men in love will make. Yet his old inhibitions prevented him from admitting his feelings to Lou openly and directly. He asked Rée to propose to her for him. But Lou turned him down—her feelings for Nietzsche and her interest in his ideas were not such as to make her wish to marry him.

This led to a complicated, ominous situation, due in part to Nietzsche's unfortunate aversion to speaking his mind directly and sincerely to Lou. A further complication was added by Rée's falling in love with her. And even though his own offer of marriage was equally unsuccessful, Rée had turned into a rival who, in addition, knew Nietzsche's innermost desires concerning the matter. It was useless of Lou to assure Nietzsche in all warmth that their friendship would remain unchanged! Conventional statements of this sort cannot disguise the difficulty of turning love (and unrequited love at that) back into a friendly teacher-pupil relationship. The situation did not improve any when Nietzsche's friends, his sister, and Lou Salomé gathered in Bayreuth that July to attend the premiere of *Parsifal*. Nietzsche had gone to Tautenburg after persuading Lou and Elisabeth to visit him there after the festival. It was obvious to him that he could not go to Bayreuth, and yet he was painfully conscious of his voluntary exclusion from the Wagner group. In a letter to Lou he wrote that he was glad not to have to be there, "and yet, if I could be near you in spirit and whisper this and that into your ear, I could even endure the *Parsifal* music." [67] And during a brief stay in Naumburg, he could not resist preparing his sister a little for *Parsifal*. "I must admit with real alarm that I've become aware once more of my close kinship with Wagner," he reported to Gast. The self-inflicted Bayreuth wounds were far from healed and would keep on hurting.

Lou and Elisabeth did come to Tautenburg together. Nietzsche, continuing his philosophical conversations with Lou, felt understood by his friend and pupil; his self-confidence grew, helped considerably by a poem she wrote, and on which he perhaps placed too much importance, because even Gast at first mistook it for a poem by Nietzsche himself.

Nietzsche's feelings for Lou were intense; but as far as she was concerned, the friendship with the lonely wanderer was never more than a profound intellectual experience such as may impress a young girl—a friendship evoking admiration and respect. Elisabeth's jealousy of the younger and more intelligent woman had already been aroused long before, and now it increased to the point of fury. Her intrigues, her gossip, her slanderous remarks about Lou were more than the others could tolerate. After Lou's departure from Tautenburg toward the end of August, Nietzsche had an open quarrel with his sister, and shortly thereafter he broke not only with her but with his mother as well. Nietzsche tried to ignore Elisabeth's gossip but without much success. In late September, upon meeting Paul Rée and Lou in Leipzig for the last time, he had a slight falling-out with Lou because of some unpleasant things he said about Rée.

Now his violently possessive sister had an easy time of it. By autumn, her constant meddling had destroyed Nietzsche's friendship with Lou and with Paul Rée. The episode was terminated by an ugly and undignified correspondence that lasted until the following year; Nietzsche felt so strongly about his embarrassing and unfair letters that later on he voiced a desire to make up for what he had done. But now Nietzsche was lonelier and unhappier than ever before. Unable to stave off his sister's attempts to win him over, he finally agreed to a superficial reconciliation; but she probably never enjoyed his full confidence again. For a long time, she forced a totally different version on the world. (It was only after her death, in 1935, that the whole extent of her intrigues and forgeries gradually became known.)

In November 1882, Nietzsche fled to Geneva and shortly thereafter to Rapallo for the winter. Once more, his state of health was so poor that he described that period to Gast as the "worst winter of my life." Insomnia and melancholy plagued him, but January and February 1883 brought a sudden euphoria that was more intense than the well-being he had experienced during the summer in Sils. A deluge of great ideas tore him out of his lethargy, and in the space of ten days Nietzsche wrote the first part of *Zarathustra*. We must add that the next two sections of the book were also composed in similar brief periods of highly intense vitality: part II in June and July 1883 at Sils-Maria, and part III in January and February 1884. Only the last section was written with interruptions during the six winter months of 1884/85 in Zurich, Mentone, and Nice.

A BOOK FOR EVERYONE AND NO ONE

In *Ecce Homo*, his last great autobiographical work, written in 1888 shortly before his breakdown, Nietzsche described the creation of *Thus Spake Zarathustra*:

"The basic concept of the work, the idea of the eternal recurrence, the highest formula of affirmation which can possibly be attained—goes back to August 1881; the idea was jotted down on a piece of paper, and below it the words: '6000 feet beyond man and time.' That day, I was walking along the lake of Silvaplana through the woods; not far from Surlei, I halted at a huge towering pyramid of logs. That was when the idea came to me.—If I count two months further back, I find an omen, an abrupt and radical change in my taste, especially in music. One might perhaps categorize all of *Zarathustra* as music—certainly a preliminary stipulation to it was to hear a renaissance in music. I was spending the spring of 1881 in Recoaro, a small mountain-spa near Vicenza, and there together with my friend and maestro Peter Gast (also one 'reborn'), I discovered that the phoenix of music flew over us, its plumage lighter and more brilliant than ever before. If, on the other hand, I count forward from that day up to the sudden delivery that came about in February 1883 under the most improbable circumstances—the closing portion, the same from which I have quoted a few lines in the preface, was completed exactly in the same holy hour in which Richard Wagner died in Venice—the time adds up to a pregnancy of eighteen months." [68]

Thus Spake Zarathustra, which many consider the culmination of Nietzsche's writings, is new and unique in its form. However, the contents embrace almost all of Nietzsche's earlier thoughts, which are focused around two new leading images: the idea of the *Übermensch* [superman] and the idea of the eternal recurrence. Thus, from the viewpoint of the contents, it is wrong to place *Zarathustra* on a lonely height. Nietzsche himself distinctly said that his previous books of aphorisms contain numerous Zarathustra thoughts.

"Upon reading *Dawn* and *The Gay Science*, I discovered that there is hardly a line in them which could not serve as an introduction to, preparation for, and commentary on *Zarathustra*. It is a fact that I wrote the commentary before the text." [69]

Even the idea (generally attributed to *Zarathustra*) that God is merely a "conjecture" and that all gods are dead, was classically formulated in *The Gay Science*:

"The greatest modern event—that 'God is dead,' that the belief in the Christian God has become unworthy of belief—is beginning to cast its first shadow across Europe." [70]

It is worth noting that Nietzsche regarded this statement merely as a diagnosis; he states the death of God but does not claim that God died through him. Ernst Bertram was thus mistaken when he wrote that Nietzsche had murdered God.

But in its form of presentation and its stylistic excellence, *Zarathustra* was second to none of Nietzsche's works. Although conceived as a philosophical treatise, the book is written entirely as pure literature. The text is studded with parables, and reads like a religious tract. Nietzsche even referred to it once as a "fifth gospel." The new philosophy is meant to be an anti-religion, it is replete with allusions to Christian dogma and even announces dithyrambically a new Dionysian philosophy. Parables and symbolic incidents are loosely connected by action that often recedes completely. The new Dionysian vitality, the development toward the great "yes sayer" Zarathustra, signified a considerable heightening of Nietzsche's aesthetic and creative will. Nature, too, is drawn in: the solitude of lofty mountains and the hills on the lake; in *Zarathustra* Nietzsche paid homage to his two favorite landscapes: the Upper Engadine and the foothills of Portofino on the bay of Rapallo.

Strangely enough, the book does not begin with the idea of the eternal recurrence, although this notion had been very much on Nietzsche's mind. Instead, the first part deals with a different motif:

"I shall teach you about the superman. Man is something that must be overcome. What have you done to overcome him? The superman is the meaning of the earth. Your will says: the superman be the meaning of the earth!

"I implore you, my brothers, remain true to the earth and do not believe those who speak to you of hopes beyond the earth! They are poisoners, whether they know it or not.

"They are contemptuous of life, moribund and poisoned, themselves and the earth is weary of them: let them pass away!

"Once, the greatest blasphemy was blasphemy of God, but God died, and the blasphemous died along with him. And now the most terrible thing of all is to blaspheme the earth and to hold the entrails of the Impenetrable in higher esteem than the meaning of the earth!

"Once, the soul was contemptuous of the body; and then this contempt was the highest—the soul wanted the body thin, ugly, starved. Thus the soul hoped to escape the body and the earth.

"What is the greatest that you could experience? It is the hour of great contempt." [71]

This is the hour in which men should begin to rise above themselves, since happiness, reason, virtue, justice, and pity are no longer meaningful. The new gospel promises a kingdom of this world and without transcendence; God being dead, man can strive only for an elevation of himself. A Dionysian religion without Dionysus.

This can be made possible only through a total affirmation of one's own life. Thus, in opposition to Christian ethics, Nietzsche extols the pleasures of the flesh, the importance of all physical existence. He pessimistically denies only the current form of the species of mankind. The fact that the Dionysian form of man has not yet materialized justifies Zarathustra's pessimism, the criticism of the status quo for the sake of future promise. For lack of space we cannot delve into the difficulties and inadequacies of this individualistic alternative religion, and we must limit ourselves to a brief outline of the rest of the book.

The true virtues of the superman are those of the warrior and the soldier. The ideal is not the lonely, alienated, sensitive scholar struggling for knowledge, but the strong person who is both vital and self-possessed. Nietzsche, normally enamored of freedom, was suddenly intoxicated by a vision of disciplinary power. A man who was not even equal to friction with his sister, who had failed physically as a soldier, and had never known a happy love, made Zarathustra preach: "Man should be trained for war, and woman for the warrior's relaxation; everything else is folly." [72] And his advice: "Are you going to women? Don't forget your whip!" [73] is easy to understand in view of a life that was driven to despair and perhaps even suicide by Lou's rejection, Elisabeth's intrigues, and the mother's stupidity. The autobiographical features of *Zarathustra* are as significant as in the other works.

Nietzsche created a life's work to find self-assurance. The aesthetics of Romanticism, whose influence lasted almost up to the middle of the twentieth century, had shaped the problem of the artist as that of an individualistic, subjective existence, and Nietzsche set himself up as an example. Along with this he managed to produce some of the finest works in German literature. Thus, for instance, *Nachtlied (Night Song)*, which he wrote in Rome for part II of *Zarathustra*:

"It is night; now all the flowing fountains speak louder. It is night; now all the songs of lovers awake. . . . A desire for love stirs in me, speaking the language of love. . . . I do not know the happiness of those who take. . . . A hunger grows out of my beauty. . . ." [74]

Such lofty diction is in keeping with the aristocratic character with which Nietzsche endows his visionary superman. His notion of an elite, which he formulated during his early study of the Greeks, is an obvious part of this conception. Actually, the idea is an Apollonian legacy; a member of the elite must be powerful and vital as well as magnanimous. And yet, power is the true goal of life: "Wherever I found life, I found the will to power; and even in the will of the servant I found the will to be master." [75]

Only in part III does Zarathustra announce and develop his theology, the dogma of the eternal recurrence of the same. This doctrine, which took compulsive hold of Nietzsche in Sils (August 1881), was apparently much harder to develop than Nietzsche originally thought. His qualms may have been of a scholarly nature, since, upon finishing *The Gay Science,* he voiced a desire to resume his studies. The notion of recurrence is developed in lurid images. In the section called *Apparition and Enigma,* Zarathustra, who has summoned up courage for his most difficult thoughts, tells a dwarf (who would be at home in Wagner's *Ring*): "Dwarf! You! Or I!" And later on: "Courage is the best assassin. . . . Courage, which attacks; after all, it kills death, to whom it says: 'Was *this* life? Very well then! Once again!' " [76] Nietzsche tells of a black serpent that slipped into the mouth of a sleeping shepherd; the only salvation is Zarathustra's desperate and distasteful advice to bite off its head. This image indicates how difficult it was for Nietzsche to endure the thought of eternal recurrence—because: "Ah! Man always returns! The little man always returns!" [77]

The entire notion is full of contradictions. On the one hand, man must overcome himself and become a superman; on the other hand, Nietzsche is certain that everything is predetermined and that just as time moves in a circle, everything is fated to recur eternally. Aren't these two basic ideas really inconsistent with one another?

Nietzsche tries to make them compatible with the aid of a dialectical notion strongly reminiscent of Hegel: Conflict unites both theses, the principle of recurrence and the demand for a superman. Recurrence contains the possibility of the enhancement and perfection of life; through recurrence the world can, to a certain extent, become richer on itself. Accordingly, the ephemeral is abolished in favor of the future, in Hegel's double interpretation of the process. Zarathustra's acceptance of tragic self-immolation is thus triumphant: "I love those who perish with all my love: for they go beyond."—And this is why he can admit: "For I love you, eternity!" [78]

This book with its astonishing wealth actually ends at the conclusion of part III. And this was Nietzsche's original plan. But soon he began contemplating additional parts. He worked gradually, completing a fourth portion, which was printed privately (1885) in a limited edition and made available to the general public only many years later, after Nietzsche's intellectual death. Trouble with his publisher may have played its part. From this point of view, *Zarathustra* is a fragment. *The Great Noon,* the closing vision of part IV, which announces a new motif, was never carried through.

By the end of part III, Nietzsche's self-assurance had increased greatly. In February 1884, he wrote to Rohde: "I tell myself that I've brought the German language to its apotheosis with this Z. After Luther and Goethe, a third step remained—; old friend and comrade, see if our language has ever known such a blend of power, suppleness, and euphony." [79]

His self-praise was unrestrained and his comparison lofty; these lines are like lightning announcing the advent of Nietzsche's final period. *Zarathustra* marks the beginning of Nietzsche's self-apotheosis—"flying on one's own wings into one's own heaven"—the desperate escape from a life destroyed by living in this world.

DISTASTEFUL EXPERIENCES

Life for Nietzsche did not become easier or more pleasant during the completion of *Zarathustra.* His health had gradually declined once more, and he had trouble with other people as well. The printing of *Zarathustra* was delayed, his publisher Schmeitzer had no confidence whatsoever in even a modest success for the book, and so it finally appeared like a stillborn child. To avoid further chagrin with Schmeitzer, Nietzsche had forty copies of part IV printed privately in 1885. Heinrich Baron von Stein, a potential disciple of Nietzsche's philosophy, had been to Sils in August 1884. But Nietzsche could not forgive him for remaining a Wagnerian, and Von Stein drifted away from him.

Nietzsche's friction with his sister and his mother never came to an end. Reconciliations gave way to new quarrels. In 1883, he wrote to Overbeck: "I don't care for my mother, and I don't like hearing my sister's voice; whenever we've been together, I've always gotten sick." [80] The following year he wrote to the same friend: "I've got to get this whole business with my family off my mind—for two years now I've been exhausting myself with kind-hearted attempts to put things in order and make peace." [81]

In summer 1883, his mother and his sister harassed him to resume his teaching career. As he had so often done before, Nietzsche gave in; he went to Leipzig to inquire about the possibilities. The bitter answer was reported to Gast: "Heinze, the current *Rektor* of the university, pulled no punches; he told me that my application would be turned down at Leipzig (and probably at all German universities); the faculty would never risk recommending me to the ministry—because of my position on Christianity and on theories of God. Bravo! This point of view inspired me with new courage." [82] Be that as it may, his visit to Leipzig was certainly a disappointment and a reaffirmation of his loneliness.

The most distasteful of all these vexations was Elisabeth Nietzsche's engagement to Dr. Bernhard Förster, a Wagnerian and a terrible political anti-Semite, who had given up his teaching post at a Berlin *Gymnasium* to devote himself to agitation. Elisabeth began tormenting her brother with anti-Jewish letters. Nietzsche was even more indignant because Förster had obviously played a part in Elisabeth's intrigues against Lou Salomé. Some nine months after the marriage (which took place in May 1885), it became clear that Elisabeth and her husband were going to emigrate to Paraguay, where Förster felt he had a mission as German "colonizer." Elisabeth convinced the world that as a result, Nietzsche's anger had waned; but it has since been proved that all of Nietzsche's letters on this point were forged by his sister at a later date, which is the reason for not quoting them here. Nietzsche's own attitude toward the Jewish question was intelligent, critical, and sovereign. Utterances of great respect for Jews predominate in his writings. And although other ideas of his may be considered proto-Fascist because of their influence, he was anything but an anti-Semite. And that his sister, of all people, had married such a man offended him deeply. In this context, the words in his last letter to Burckhardt, written after Nietzsche's breakdown, are significant: ". . . all anti-Semites gotten rid of."

6 FINAL PERIOD AND BREAKDOWN

The years preceding Nietzsche's collapse contain few outward events. The philosopher seemed to have found a rhythm; he spent his summers in Sils, his winters in the south, especially in Nice, after 1888 also in Turino. He made an unsuccessful attempt to promote Gast's musical work, but the two men drifted apart slightly. Of much more serious consequence was an almost groundless dissension with Rohde—symptomatic of increasing deterioration of health, loneliness, and irritability.

In September 1887, Deussen, who had just become professor of philosophy, brought his wife along on a visit to Sils. Nietzsche told Gast about the visit, referring to it as "funny and touching"; but he had great respect and feelings of friendship for Deussen, whom he hadn't seen in such a long time. Deussen did a pen-and-ink sketch of him, and in his memoirs he included a detailed impression of Nietzsche and his life in Sils:

"On a beautiful autumn day, my wife and I, having come from Chiavenna, climbed over the Pass of Maloja, and soon Sils-Maria lay before us. My heart was beating as I found my friend after fourteen years of separation and embraced him, deeply moved. But what changes had taken place in him. Where was the proud posture, the supple walk, the fluent speech? He dragged along with great difficulty, lopping to one side, and his speech was frequently heavy and halting. Perhaps it wasn't his good day. 'Dear friend,' his voice was melancholy and he pointed at a cloud drifting by, 'I have to have a blue sky above me to collect my thoughts.' Next, he led us to his favorite spots. I distinctly recall a stretch of turf on the edge of a cliff, high above a mountain brook that rushed along at the bottom. 'This,' he said, 'is my favorite place for lying down, and here I have my best thoughts.' We had taken rooms at the modest *Hotel zur Alpenrose,* where Nietzsche always ate his lunch, usually consisting of a single chop or the like. We retired there for an hour's rest. No sooner was the hour up than our friend was at the door, tenderly asking if we were still tired, apologizing for coming too early, etc. I mention this, because such over-solicitousness and over-considerateness, untypical of the earlier Nietzsche, seemed characteristic of his present condition. The next morning, he took me over to his place, or as he put it, his lair. It was a simple room in a farmhouse, three minutes from the roadside. Nietzsche had rented it during the season for one franc a day. The furniture was as simple as could be. To one side, I saw his books, most of which were familiar to me from before, a rustic table with a coffee cup on it, egg-shells, manuscripts, toilet articles, all in great disorder, which spread over a bootjack with boots attached, to the still unmade bed. Everything pointed to careless domestics and to a patient master who put up with anything. In the afternoon we set out again, and Nietzsche accompanied me as far as the neighboring village, one hour downstream. Here, he repeated the somber forebodings that were to be realized so soon. When we bade one another farewell, tears rushed to his eyes, something I had never known in him before." [83]

THE FINAL WORKS

Any dealings with Nietzsche's later output involve scholarly controversy which must be mentioned, even in a biographical description devoid of literary or far-reaching aims. The list of books produced after *Thus Spake Zarathustra,* in the last four years of Nietzsche's creative work, is not the subject of disputation: *Beyond Good and Evil* (1886); *Toward a Genealogy of Morals* (1887); *The Wagner Case; Dionysus Dithyrambs; Twilight of the Idols; The Antichrist; Ecce Homo;* and *Nietzsche contra Wagner* in the year preceding his collapse. What is controversial is *The Will to Power,* whose renown is second only to *Zarathustra's.* In 1906, when the first edition appeared, Elisabeth Förster-Nietzsche wrote: "In late winter 1888, my brother finished the total conception of his magnum opus, *The Will to Power.*" All that we know with certainty is that the 1067 aphorisms in this book are from posthumous material

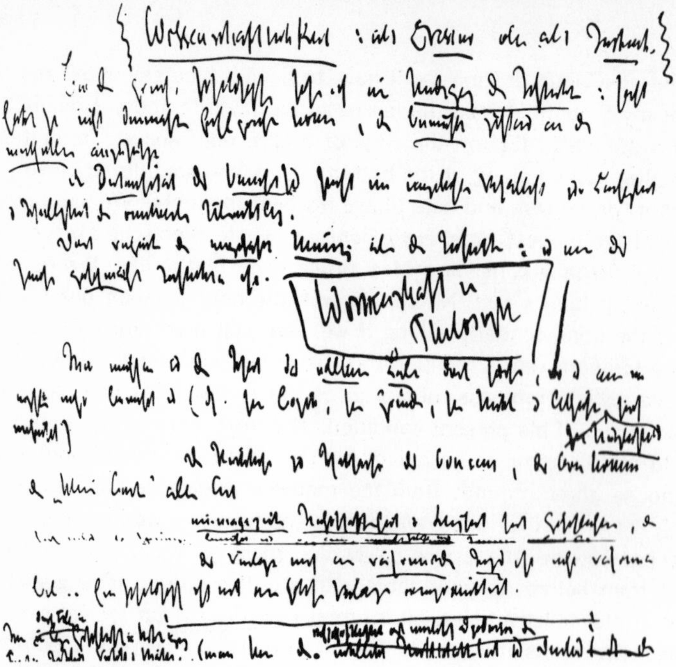

Notes for The Will to Power.

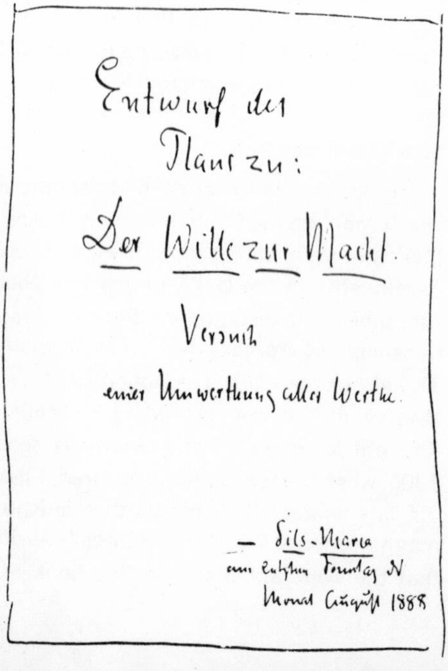

Entwurf des
Plans zu:
Der Wille zur Macht.
Versuch
einer Umwerthung aller Werthe.

— Sils-Maria
am letzten Sonntag des
Monat August 1888

Draft of title page
for The Will to Power.

Paul Deussen.

Elisabeth Förster-Nietzsche, 1916.

and were put together by editors who were under Elisabeth's influence. But this structuring of the work finds little support in relevant plans and comments of Nietzsche's. After completing part III of *Zarathustra*, he had written to Gast: ". . . the next six years will be taken up with working out a scheme, with which I have outlined my 'philosophy.' It is going well and promisingly." [84]

The fact remains, however, that this major work was not conceived in any recognizable, unified form. And whether Nietzsche himself would have chosen the title *The Will to Power* remains open to question. For him, the phrase "The Will to Power" was the designation for a fundamental principle to which all of life submits. Quite obviously Nietzsche had intended to develop this philosophical principle more fully, as is shown by numerous notes and drafts. But we actually have nothing more than concepts, notes, sketches, and do not know which material Nietzsche would have selected for a work dealing with "The Will to Power." The existing volume bearing this title is an arbitrary arrangement by the editors. It has long since been established and become common knowledge that Nietzsche's posthumous works were edited carelessly. Karl Schlechta, who demonstrated the numerous forgeries by Nietzsche's sister, places the entire blame on her, whereas Erich F. Podach is probably correct in also attacking the elite of renowned German professors who for decades played a part in, or at least tolerated, the editorial sloppiness and the legend it helped create. As a result, Karl Schlechta, in his excellent new edition of Nietzsche's complete works, was guided by a radical but understandable purism in reorganizing the literary remains of the 1880s and rejecting both the title *The Will to Power* and the structure (neither of which goes back to Nietzsche) on the basis of sound philological principles. Outstanding Nietzsche scholars like Karl Löwith have protested against this. It is curious, nevertheless, that a book with such an enormous influence should now dissolve into a mass of disconnected aphorisms. Yet one has to give Schlechta his due; rather than mutilating Nietzsche, he salvaged the posthumous works from the violence done them by earlier editors. The new, unstructured arrangement does not, in any event, interfere with the objective study of Nietzsche's work.

The literary remains contained passages of grandiose power; but extensive as the posthumous works may be, they include few fundamental ideas that cannot be found in and developed out of Nietzsche's established *oeuvre*. Ever since *Human, All-Too-Human*, Nietzsche had been philosophizing in the form of aphorisms, which, as we have seen, was in keeping with his work methods. He made selections from the wealth of notes and sketches, often arranging the material by association, occasionally using some of it more than once, and undoubtedly leaving out and even totally rejecting certain passages. Thus, on the basis of the literary remains, we can claim that from 1882 to 1888 Nietzsche was occupied with the group of themes which was erroneously gathered together in earlier editions under the working title, *The Will to Power*. Although Nietzsche may have referred to *Zarathustra* as a *Vorhof*, a forecourt, his alleged magnum opus never assumed recognizable form. A study of the works written in the final four years is obfuscated by something else; as Nietzsche's state of health altered, his self-opinion and his belief in his mission increased beyond all measure. Whether or not he really did spend only ten days on each of the first three parts of *Zarathustra*, Nietzsche was now intent on claiming similarly short geneses for his late works in order to create an impression of visionary inspiration. Considering his method of writing, it was certainly not difficult to make a selection from the great hoard of ever-increasing aphoristic material and then work it into a manuscript and prepare the final draft within a few weeks. It is hard to judge when and where his unrelenting illness influenced either the contents or the form. From what we know of his case, we cannot establish the exact point at which the destruction that claimed his mind made his work dubious. However, according to Podach's recent study on "Nietzsche's Works at the Time of His Breakdown," it is clear that the mental collapse left a decisive mark on everything Nietzsche wrote during his second trip to Turino from September 21, 1888, to early January 1889: *Nietzsche contra Wagner, The Antichrist, Ecce Homo*, and *Dionysus Dithyrambs*.

Yet it was these works which, next to the controversial *Will to Power*, have always exerted a magical fascination on Nietzsche's more enthusiastic followers. The philosopher was thus subjected to the same—albeit occasionally fruitful—misunderstanding as Hölderlin, whose admirers began to regard his final poetry as revelations of a very particular sort. Purely speculative interpretations can be philosophically legitimate. But a biographer has to observe more caution.

In 1886 and 1887, Nietzsche had all his major works republished, authorizing them with new prefaces. Omitting only *The Untimely Meditations*, he even included *The Birth of Tragedy*, although he had long since rejected its positions. This fact illuminates the great extent to which Nietzsche viewed his entire output as a unit. The major early themes remained and the reader seeking initiation into Nietzsche's writ-

ings can temporarily avoid the complicated problems of the posthumous works. Nietzsche's thoughts can be understood and developed
from the works he authorized to be published. All the post-*Zarathustra*
writings, however, accentuate a series of ideas which must play a
decisive part in any portrait of Nietzsche. The following survey of
Nietzsche's last period is therefore oriented not so much on individual
works as on the important themes of the closing years.

NIHILISM AS THE LOGIC OF DECADENCE

The development of Nietzsche's immoralism came early and was not
without consistency. His rejection of Christianity was followed by a
Dionysian philosophy initially determined by aesthetic views. But during
Nietzsche's first few years at Basel, the primacy of aesthetic existence
gave way, under Burckhardt's influence, to the historical personality;
the aspect of power became essential to any judgment of history. This
was the first time that Nietzsche took a position "beyond good and
evil," by denying the justifiability of moral principles and human judgment of right and wrong. The tendency pursued in an early work, *On
Truth and Falsehood in the Supramoral Sense,* was thus continued and
strengthened. The final writings were governed by the idea that life
and the world are devoid of any recognizable meaning, that all past
attempts at giving them meaning were merely human and very much
open to criticism, and that man must therefore be all the more intent on
mastering his life in a meaningless world. In the summer of 1887, he
wrote: "The most extreme form of nihilism would be the realization
that every belief and any faith in any truth are necessarily wrong,
because a true world does not exist. Ergo: a perspective illusion." [85]
And further on: "Let us think this thought in its most terrible form:
existence such as it is, devoid of aim or meaning, yet unavoidably recur-
rent, without a finale in nothingness: 'the eternal recurrence.' This is
the extreme form of nihilism: nothingness ('meaninglessness') for-
ever!" [86] But nihilism appears as a paradox symptom:

"Nihilism as a normal phenomenon can be a symptom of growing
strength or growing weakness:

"In part, that the power to create and to will has grown to such an
extent that it no longer needs these total interpretations and attributions
of meaning ('personal missions,' the state, etc.);

"In part, that even the creative power to create meaning slackens,
and disappointment becomes the prevailing condition. The inability to
believe in a 'meaning,' 'non-belief.' " [87]

Nihilism is thus both a strength and a weakness. A strength inasmuch as our cognition perceives in the development of nihilism a necessary process, by which all ideological counterfeiting is exposed, and all traditional values are withdrawn from circulation. At the same time, nihilism is a symptom of weakness: because its development implies the exhaustion and failure of all culture thus far. This weakness, which Nietzsche called decadence, is the cause of nihilism, which is thereby the result of decadence—its very logic, as Nietzsche once put it. Decadence, however, is like a destiny; a process of decline cannot be halted. It is obvious that Nietzsche was strongly influenced by biological considerations. Only a step remains to the thesis of the right of the strongest, the demand that everything about to fall must be given a push, that every doom or downfall is a joyful, positive event—a thesis championed by Zarathustra and recurring over and over again. The idea of *The Will to Power* developed from nihilism is thus basically a revaluation of all values:

"Let no one misunderstand the sense of the title for this gospel of the future. *The Will to Power. Attempt at a Revaluation of All Values.* This formula expresses a counter-movement with regard to principle and mission; a movement which at some future time will replace all perfect nihilism; but which presupposes it logically and psychologically; which can only come after and from that nihilism. Why is the coming of nihilism necessary? Because our previous values themselves have their ultimate consequence in nihilism; because nihilism is the logic of our great values and ideas thought out to the end—because we must live through nihilism in order to discover what the value of these 'values' was. . . . We need new values at some point." [88]

Even nihilism as a necessary, non-deferrable event is no more a value in itself than good or evil; nihilism is diagnosed with the clarity and acuteness to which Nietzsche owes his fame—whatever opinion one may have of the prognostic portion of his doctrine. If ascribing meaning is the same as establishing values, then observing the world with a mind devoid of values involves a nihilistic attitude. In that case, overestimation of historical development or treatment as well as modern natural science are nihilistic forms of expression of our specific world-behavior. The diagnosis is correct. But is the recommended therapy any good?

THE WILL TO POWER AS A THERAPEUTIC PRINCIPLE

Whether or not Nietzsche really wanted to elaborate his doctrine of the Will to Power in a magnum opus, the idea itself is one of his essential themes in the 1880s. We may place the point of departure in a need which the philosopher recognized at an early time—the need to replace Schopenhauer's abstract will with a concrete principle. This occurred in *Beyond Good and Evil*—and not only there—in terms of biological notions:

"Supposing finally that we managed to explain all our instincts as the development and ramification of a basic form of the will, to wit, the will to power, as is my thesis; supposing that we could trace back all organic functions to this will to power and find in it the solution to the problem of procreation and nourishment—this is a problem—we would thereby have acquired the right to call all active energy unequivocally the Will to Power. The world as seen from the inside, the world determined and designated in terms of its 'intelligible character,' would be this very 'Will to Power' and nothing else." [89]

Quotations of this sort are legion. Even nourishment is supposedly just a consequence of the insatiable Will to Power, which is simply "the unexhausted, generating life-will," the "principle of life." It is also the "primal fact of all history" and in creative people it is sublimated in art, as the "intoxication of the great will that craves art." According to *Twilight of the Idols:*

"The sublimest feeling of power and security is expressed in that which has great style. The power which no longer needs any proof; which scornfully refuses to please; which answers with difficulty; which feels no witness around itself; which lives without awareness of the fact that there is opposition against it; which is self-contained, fatalistic, a law among laws: This speaks of itself as a great style." [90]

The same aphorisms contain Nietzsche's old aversion to the Socratic method, nay, to rationality and cognition. The blind, totally instinctual will is the principle of not only life but the creative act as well. Insights formulated a generation before Freud and questioning all traditional values, yet they could not be what they were meant to be: the prelude to a philosophy of the future.

THE IDEA OF AN ELITE

The revaluation of all values itself posits new values. And this is what makes it seem revolutionary and original. Nietzsche, sick, lonely, misunderstood, and a failure in his lifetime, celebrates the victory of strength. From the Dionysian philosophy of *The Birth of Tragedy* through *Thus Spake Zarathustra* and until the very end, Nietzsche's thoughts were marked by an inclination toward violence—a glorification of violence in many different forms. The new gospel is a justification of the physically and mentally strong, who together will form the future power elite. A select aristocracy who can unhesitatingly accept the sacrifice of the weak and enslaved. The great man, the higher individual, aristocrat, tyrannic ruler, hero—he alone has the highest value. Great men are the sole apology of human society and its history:

"Revolution, chaos, and the misery of nations are insignificant, in my view, compared with the misery of great individuals in their development. . . . The collective misery of all these small beings adds up to nothing except in the feelings of powerful men." [91] To offer a concrete example: "It was the revolution that made Napoleon possible, this is its justification. For a similar reward, we would have to wish the anarchistic collapse of our entire civilization. Napoleon made nationalism possible; this is his excuse." [92]

Nietzsche wanted to be the self-styled prophet of a tiny elite of the future, privileged to be the ruling class. But its path would be one of severity toward itself as well:

"For those people who are of any concern to me, I wish suffering, loneliness, disease, ill-treatment, degradation—I want them to know the feeling of a profound self-contempt, the tormenting lack of self-confidence, the misery of the vanquished. I have no pity for them, because I wish them the only thing in existence that can prove if a man has value or not—the ability to hold his own." [93]

Steadfastness as a watchword for its own sake may be viewed as a basic principle of existentialist thought in the twentieth century. Here too, with his concept of the lonely greatness of the aristocratic being, Nietzsche was a decisive pioneer of later philosophy, especially in Germany. The powerful are the aristocrats: "beasts of prey," for whom the motto "live dangerously" is the key to the secret of the good life. In contrast, the moral code of the slave, the herd, is the expression of weakness.

"The pleasant feelings infused in us by men who are good, well-meaning, and just (as opposed to the tension and fear inspired by the great, new man) constitute our personal sense of security and equality; the herd-animal exalts herd-nature, and thereby experiences well-being. The judgment of this well-being disguises itself with fine words—and thus 'morality' is born." [94]

Nietzsche, indulging (in *The Antichrist*) in violent outbursts against Christianity, ventures at the same time into the realm of theological speculation. His comments, whose aphoristic form has a deceptively acute effect, would impress any believer: "It is wrong to the point of nonsense to see in any 'faith,' like the faith in deliverance through Christ, the sign of Christ; only Christian practice, a life like His who died on the cross, is Christianity. . . ." [95] And suddenly, harmonious chords burst forth in that mystic and romantic mode so characteristic of Nietzsche's background:

"The 'kingdom of heaven' is a state of the heart—and not something that comes 'above the earth' or 'after death.' The entire concept of natural death is missing in the gospels. Death is not a bridge, a transition; it is missing because it belongs to a completely different world, a specious world, a world useful only as a sign. The 'hour of death' is not a Christian concept—the 'hour,' time, physical life and its crises do not exist for the bearer of the 'joyous tiding.' . . . The 'Kingdom of God' is not a matter of expectation; it has no past and no future, it will not come in a 'millennium'—it is the experience of a heart; it exists everywhere, it exists nowhere. . . ." [96]

The reader who singles out thoughts of this kind, and makes Nietzsche the prototype of the modern God-feeling atheist, should not forget the general tenor of Nietzsche's statements on Christianity. Nietzsche's immoralism remained to the very end an extreme contrast to Christian ideas. This cannot be denied, even if we are to regard the almost unbalanced conclusion of *The Antichrist* as a sign of approaching insanity.

FINAL ACCOUNT

This last phase is like an attempt at clarification of everything that Nietzsche had ever thought or intended. Yet we cannot take a premonition of the end as the motive. In 1888 Nietzsche went through a final, unprecedented transport of creativity; yet his writings reveal the ghostly shadows of the coming night. Wagner died in 1883, and five years later Nietzsche tried once more to come to grips with the man to whom he owed a decisive debt and whom he always viewed as his most important intellectual opponent. Thus, in 1888, Nietzsche wrote the pamphlet *The Wagner Case*; this not sufficing, he collected all the old arguments of his earlier writings against his supposed rival and put them together in a manuscript entitled *Nietzsche contra Wagner,* which he finished by Christmas of the same year. It was to be his final piece of work. In *The Wagner Case,* Nietzsche's hatred had already exploded and by playing off Bizet against Wagner, Nietzsche let jealous resentment interfere with his usual excellent sense of musical quality. Nietzsche even managed to attend twenty performances of *Carmen.* But *Ecce Homo,* probably the strangest autobiography ever written, shows that Nietzsche's musical taste had altered through and through: "Let me say a word to first-rate ears on what I expect of music. Music should be cheerful and deep like an October afternoon. Whimsical, gay, tender, a sweet little female, underhanded and charming. . . ." [97] Wagner is put down completely, he is an "actor," an artist whose sole merit is to be found in details and minor touches, a genius manqué. Nietzsche's critique assumes pathological proportions:

"Wagner's art is sick. The problems he presents on stage—pure hysteria—, the convulsive quality of his passions, his hypersensitivity, his taste which constantly demands sharper spices, his instability disguised as principles, the choice of his heroes and heroines, viewed as physiological types (a gallery of invalids!): all of it presents a portrait of disease that leaves no doubt. *Wagner est une névrose.* (Wagner is a neurosis.)" [98]

Nietzsche was unwittingly giving Wagner features of his own condition.

7 THE END: DIONYSUS VS. THE MAN ON THE CROSS

On January 3, 1889, in Turino, Nietzsche mailed three messages. One of them said: ". . . in the last few days, a certain divine buffoon has just completed the *Dionysus Dithyrambs*. . . ." [99] He had written these poems between 1884 and 1888, and now he suddenly finished the final copy. They are a cryptic portrait of his friendship with Cosima Wagner, who appears as Ariadne, and reveal more about Nietzsche's condition resulting from his own break with his Bayreuth friends than anything else. Thus, *Ariadne's Lament* goes in part:

> No!
> Come back!
> (. . .)
> All my tears run
> their course to you
> and my heart's last flame
> blazes for you.
> Oh come back
> my unknown God! my anguish!
> my last happiness!

And in *Ecce Homo*, recalling the *Night Song* of *Zarathustra*, Nietzsche writes: "The like has never been composed, felt, suffered before: only a god, a Dionysus, can suffer thus. The answer to such a dithyramb of solar solitude in light would be Ariadne. . . . Who besides me knows what Ariadne is! . . ." He revealed this knowledge to Burckhardt in a last letter written in madness: "The rest for Frau Cosima . . . Ariadne." [100]

The staccato beauty of the Dionysus Dithyrambs, put out by Peter Gast in 1891, has always delighted and enchanted those who worship Nietzsche blindly. These poems are in no way the revelation they have often been called, but do show the devastating anguish of Nietzsche's final productive years. He tried in vain to conjure up and rise into something contrary to his own nature, something he was not and could never be. All that remained for him was a promise—the promise of his own philosophy, to which he could cling to the very end:

"Dionysus vs. the 'Man on the Cross': there is your contrast. In the former case, it is to be the way leading to sacred existence; in the latter, existence is sacred enough to justify tremendous suffering. The tragic man affirms the most bitter suffering: he is strong, solid, and transfiguring enough; the Christian man denies even the happiest lot on earth: he is weak, poor, and disinherited enough to suffer life in every form. The God on the cross is a curse on life, a hint to deliver oneself from it—Dionysus, cut into shreds, is a promise of life; it will be reborn eternally and come back from destruction." [101]

In 1888, his last conscious year, Nietzsche once more reached a new station in his endless wanderings. After spending the winter in Nice, he came to Turino on April 5, and was so taken with the city that he later referred to it in a letter to his mother as a "true gift of fortune." His arrival was accompanied by some excellent news: Georg Brandes had announced a lecture course on the German philosopher Friedrich Nietzsche at the University of Copenhagen. These tidings were a premonition of coming renown that Nietzsche himself would never know. His health was once again extremely poor in 1888. He felt miserable apart from brief phases of illuminated frenzy. That summer he went to his beloved Sils-Maria for the seventh time. On September 21, he returned to Turino, and during the next few weeks and months, as he worked on his final manuscripts, his life rapidly became more and more peculiar. At the same time, his self-image lost all sense of proportion. Ecce Homo bears permanent testimony to this self-glorification. We know little about the time between Christmas 1888 and the first week of the new year. Undoubtedly there was clear forewarning of the outbreak of Nietzsche's derangement. He told Overbeck that he intended to take the destinies of the world into his own hands:

"I am just working on a memorandum for the courts of Europe for the

Nun umgiebt ich
näher mir süsser Sicherheit
wärmer der Sonne Blick:
– Glüht nicht das Eis meines Gipfels noch?
Silbern, leicht, ein Fisch
schwimmt nun mein Nachen hinaus ...

From the Dionysus Dithyrambs, *1886.*

Peter Gast.

Meinem maestro Pietro

Singe mir ein neues Lied: die Welt ist verklärt
und alle Himmel freuen sich

Nietzsche's postcard to Peter Gast, from Turino, January 4, 1889.

Nietzsche, after the outbreak of his illness, with his mother.

purpose of an anti-German league. I want to strangle the 'Reich' in an iron shirt and provoke it to a war of desperation. My hands won't be free until I get them on the young Kaiser and all his paraphernalia." [102]

Nietzsche wrote this on December 28; and on the last day of the year, he answered a postcard from Peter Gast with the following lines: "Ah, my friend! What a moment!—When your card arrived what did I do. . . . It was the famed Rubicon.—I no longer know my address: let us assume that for the time being it will be the Palazzo del Quirinale." [103]

On January 4, 1889, he sent off another postcard:

"To my maestro Pietro.

Sing me a new song: the world is transfigured and all the heavens are glad.

The Man on the Cross" [104]

Nietzsche had reached the ultimate stage of megalomania. His breakdown came on January 3, in Turino, on Piazza Carlo Alberto. Upon leaving his house, Nietzsche saw a brutal coachman mistreating his horse. Bursting into tears and wailing, he threw himself on the animal's neck and collapsed. A few days later Overbeck brought him to the Basel Sanatorium. The doctor noted: "Pupils different, the right one larger than the left one, very phlegmatic reaction. Strabismus convergens. Strong myopia. Tongue thickly coated; no deviation, no tremor, facial nerves barely disturbed; . . . patellar reflexes heightened; . . . no real sense of being ill, feels very good and is in high spirits. Claims to have been sick for the past week and often to have had violent headaches; he says he had several attacks, during which patient felt uncommonly well and in high spirits, and wanted to embrace and kiss all the people on the street, and climb up the walls." [105]

In mid-January, his mother came for him, and together with Overbeck they journeyed to Jena, where Nietzsche was taken into Professor Binswanger's nursing-home. The diagnosis in Basel was "Paralysis progressiva." Thereafter Nietzsche's mental derangement increased, while he himself calmed down and his megalomania decreased. His mother moved to Jena, and in March 1890 she was permitted to take him into her care. Deussen saw him for the last time on Nietzsche's fiftieth birthday on October 15, 1894 and gave the following account:

"I came early in the morning, since I had to leave Jena shortly thereafter. His mother brought him in, I wished him many happy returns, told him that he was fifty years old today, and gave him a bouquet of flowers. He understood none of this. Only the flowers seemed to arouse his interest for a moment, then they too lay there unnoticed." [106]

Nietzsche's insanity lasted for more than a decade. After his mother's death, in 1897, his sister took over. Widowed, Elisabeth Förster-Nietzsche had returned from Paraguay and moved into a house in Weimar. There she not only watched over her mentally ill brother, but also collected his books, manuscripts, and jottings. Even before her brother died, she initiated the misrepresentation which gave rise to the Nietzsche legend. Nietzsche himself never knew anything about it. He died on August 25, 1900, and was buried next to his father in the graveyard at Röcken. Only a few years later, the fame of the greatest diagnostician of European nihilism began to spread around the world.

CHRONOLOGY

1844	October 15: Friedrich Nietzsche was born to the pastor of Röcken near Lützen in the province of Saxony.
1849	July 30: Nietzsche's father died.
1850	Nietzsche's family settles in Naumburg.
1858	October to September 1864: Nietzsche attends the *Gymnasium* of Schulpforta near Naumburg.
1864	October: Nietzsche enrolls at the University of Bonn to study theology and classical letters.
1865	October: Nietzsche transfers to the University of Leipzig. His first encounter with Schopenhauer's magnum opus.
1866	He and Erwin Rohde become friends.
1867-1868	Military service.
1868	November 8: First meeting with Richard Wagner, in Leipzig.
1869	February: Nietzsche receives a chair of classical letters at the University of Basel.
	May 17: Nietzsche's first visit to Wagner's house in Tribschen near Lucerne.
	May 28: Nietzsche's introductory lecture at Basel on *Homer and Classical Philology*. His first meetings with Jacob Burckhardt.
1869-1871	Nietzsche writes *The Birth of Tragedy* (published in early January 1872).
1870	March: Nietzsche becomes a full professor.
	August: Nietzsche becomes a nurse in the Franco-Prussian War; falls gravely ill.
	October: return to Basel. Beginning of his friendship with the theologian Franz Overbeck.
1872	February-March: Basel lectures: *On the Future of Our Educational Institutions* (published posthumously).
	April: The Wagners leave Tribschen.
	May 22: The cornerstone is laid for the Bayreuth *Festspielhaus*, Wagner and Nietzsche in Bayreuth.
1873	The first *Untimely Meditation: David Strauss, the Confessor and the Writer*.
	The second *Untimely Meditation: The Use and Abuse of History for Life* (published in 1874).
	The fragment: *Philosophy in the Tragic Age of the Greeks* (published posthumously).
1874	The third *Untimely Meditation: Schopenhauer as an Educator*.
1875-1876	The fourth *Untimely Meditation: Richard Wagner in Bayreuth*.
1875	October: Nietzsche meets the musician Peter Gast (Heinrich Köselitz).
1876	August: First Bayreuth festival. Nietzsche in Bayreuth.
	September: Nietzsche becomes friendly with the psychologist Paul Rée. Nietzsche's health declines.
	October: Leave of absence for reasons of health from the University of Basel. Winter in Sorrento with Rée and Malwida von Meysenbug.

October-November: Final meeting of Nietzsche and Wagner in Sorrento.

1876-1878 Part one of *Human, All-Too-Human.*

1878 January 3: Wagner's last communication with Nietzsche: "Parsifal."

1879 May: Nietzsche's last letter to Wagner with the manuscript of *Human, All-Too-Human.*

Nietzsche falls gravely ill. Resigns from the University of Basel.

1880 *The Wanderer and His Shadow, Human, All-Too-Human, Part IV.*

March-June: First visit to Venice.

As of November: winter in Genoa.

1880-1881 *Dawn.*

1881 First summer in Sils-Maria.

November 27: In Genoa, Nietzsche hears Bizet's *Carmen* for the first time.

1881-1882 *The Gay Science.*

1882-1888 Attempt at a Revaluation of All Values.

1882 March: Trip to Sicily.

April-November: Friendship with Lou Salomé.

As of November: winter in Rapallo.

1883 February: in Rapallo, Nietzsche writes Part One of *Thus Spake Zarathustra* (printed in 1883).

June: Part Two of *Zarathustra.*

December: Nietzsche goes to Nice to spend his first winter there.

1884 January: In Nice, Nietzsche writes Part Three of *Zarathustra* (printed in 1884).

August: Heinrich von Stein visits Sils-Maria.

November 1884–February 1885: In Mentone and Nice, Nietzsche writes Part Four of *Zarathustra* (printed privately in 1885).

1884-1885 *Beyond Good and Evil* (published in 1886).

1886 May-June: Nietzsche's last meeting with Erwin Rohde in Leipzig.

1887 *Genealogy of Morals.*

November 11: Last letter to Erwin Rohde.

1888 April: Nietzsche's first visit to Turino. Georg Brandes gives a lecture course at the University of Copenhagen "On the German Philosopher Friedrich Nietzsche."

May-August: *The Wagner Case.* Nietzsche completes the *Dionysus Dithyrambs.*

August-September: *Twilight of the Idols* (published in Jan. 1889).

September: *The Antichrist. Attempt at a Critique of Christianity* (Revaluation of All Values, I).

October-November: *Ecce Homo* (published in 1908).

December: *Nietzsche contra Nietzsche. Documents of a Psychologist* (first published in the *Works*).

1889 During January, mental breakdown in Turino.

1897 Easter: death of Nietzsche's mother.—Nietzsche and his sister settle in Weimar.

1900 August 25: Nietzsche dies in Weimar.

NOTES

Note—All quotations throughout this volume have been newly translated. Thus no page references can be given for any English edition of the works quoted from, and the following therefore refer to German editions. The source material of the original German version of this work is the three-volume edition of Nietzsche's works edited by Karl Schlechte and published by Carl Hanser Verlag (3rd edition, 1966), unless otherwise noted. A selected list of Nietzsche's works available in English is included for the reader's convenience.

1 Ecce Homo—(II, p. 1099.)
2 E. Förster-Nietzsche, The Life of Friedrich Nietzsche; Vol. I: The Young Nietzsche (Das Leben Friedrich Nietzsches; Leipzig 1913), p. 14.
3 Autobiographical writings From 1856-69—(III, p. 21.)
4 The Young Nietzsche (Der junge Nietzsche) (Op.cit., p.46.)
5 Autobiographical Writings From 1856-69—(III, p. 117/18.)
6 P. Deussen, Reminiscences of Friedrich Nietzsche (Erinnerungen an Friedrich Nietzsche), Leipzig 1901, p. 4.
7 Autobiographical Writings From 1856-69—(III, p. 96 ff.)
8 Autobiographical Writings From 1856-69—(III, p. 151.)
9 Letters—(III, p. 945.)
10 Friedrich Nietzsche, Works and Letters: complete historical-critical edition, Munich 1938, Letters, Vol. I, Letter Nr. 260, p. 301. (Werke und Briefe, hist. krit. Gesamtausg.)
11 Autobiographical Writings From 1856-69—(III, p. 135.)
12 Autobiographical Writings From 1856-69—(III, p. 133 ff.)
13 Autobiographical Writings From 1856-69—(III, p. 145 ff.)
14 Letters—(III, p. 999.)
15 Letters—(III, p. 970.)
16 Letters—(III, p. 982.)
17 Letters—(III, p. 1004.)
18 Letters—(III, p. 1019.)
19 Letters—(III, p. 1012.)
20 Ecce Humo (II, p. 1090.)
21 The Birth of Tragedy—(I, p. 11.)
22 The Birth of Tragedy—(I, p. 9-10.)
23 The Birth of Tragedy—(I, p. 23.)
24 The Birth of Tragedy—(I, p. 24.)
25 The Birth of Tragedy—(I, p. 64.)
26 Letters by Cosima Wagner to Friedrich Nietzsche, published by Thierbach, Weimar 1938, Vol. II, p. 17. (Briefe Cosima Wagners an Friedrich Nietzsche, Hersgg. von Thierbach.)
27 Letters—(III, p. 1058.)
28 Wilamowitz, Philology of the Future (Zukunftsphilologie), Berlin 1872, p. 23.
29 Thus Spake Zarathustra—(II, p. 380.)
30 On the Future of Our Educational Institutions—1st lecture (III, p. 194.)
31 On the Future of Our Educational Institutions—2nd lecture (III, p. 212.)
32 On the Future of Our Educational Institutions—5th lecture (III, p. 261.)
33 Philosophy in the Tragic Age of the Greeks —(III, p. 356.)
34 On Truth and Falsehood in the Supramoral Sense—(III, p. 314.)
35 Untimely Meditations I: David Strauss—(I, p. 137.)
36 Untimely Meditations II: The Use and Abuse of History—(I, p. 281.)
37 Musarion edition (Vol. VII, p. 71.)
38 Letters—(III, p. 1090.)
39 Letters—(III, p. 1087.)
40 Untimely Meditations IV: Richard Wagner in Bayreuth—(I, p. 415.)
41 Untimely Meditations IV: Richard Wagner in Bayreuth—(I, p. 422.)
42 Untimely Meditations IV: Richard Wagner in Bayreuth—(I, p. 426.)
43 Untimely Meditations IV: Richard Wagner in Bayreuth—(I, p. 434.)
44 Op.cit.: Wagner and Nietzsche at the time of their friendship—Munich 1915, p. 213 (E. Förster-Nietzsche.)
45 Collected Letters, 5 volumes, Berlin and Leipzig 1900 ff. Letter of August 1, 1875 (Friedrich Nietzsche, Gesammelte Briefe.)
46 Letters—(III, p. 1123.)
47 Wagner and Nietzsche, op.cit., p. 240.
48 Letter to his sister, August 1, 1876—(III, p. 1368.)
49 Nietzsche Contra Wagner—(II, p. 1054.)
50 Letters—(III, p. 1123.)
51 Letters—(III, p. 1117.)
52 Letters—(III, p. 1103ff.)
53 Friedrich Nietzsche, Collected Letters—op.cit., Letter of July 6, 1879.
54 Letters—(III, p. 1131ff.)
55 Musarion edition (Vol. 21, p. 88.)
56 Human, All-Too-Human, (I, p. 459) (Aphorism 16.)
57 Human, All-Too-Human, (I, p. 506) (Aphorism 99.)
58 Human, All-Too-Human, (I, p. 582.)
59 Human, All-Too-Human, (I, p. 730) (Aphorism 638.)
60 Human, All-Too-Human, (I, p. 852) (Aphorism 324.)
61 Human, All-Too-Human, (I, p. 440.)
62 Letters (Letter of August 14, 1881)—(III, p. 1173.)
63 Letters—(III, p. 1170.)
64 Letters—(III, p. 1172.)
65 Letters—(III, p. 1180.)
66 The Gay Science, Book IV—(II, p. 161.)
67 L. Andréas-Salomé, Friedrich Nietzsche in his works, Dresden, p. 80.
68 Ecce Homo—(II, p. 1128ff.)
69 Letters—(III, p. 1218.)

70 The Gay Science, Book IV—(II, p. 202.)
71 Thus Spake Zarathustra—(II, p. 280.)
72 Thus Spake Zarathustra—(II, p. 328.)
73 Thus Spake Zarathustra—(II, p. 330.)
74 Thus Spake Zarathustra—(II, p. 362.)
75 Thus Spake Zarathustra—(II, p. 371.)
76 Thus Spake Zarathustra—(II, p. 406.)
77 Thus Spake Zarathustra—(II, p. 465.)
78 Thus Spake Zarathustra—(II, p. 474.)
79 Letters—(III, p. 1251.)
80 Letter to Overbeck, March 1883—(III, p. 1373.)
81 Letter to Overbeck, May 1884—(III, p. 1374.)
82 Nietzsche's letters to Peter Gast, Berlin 1929.
83 P. Deussen, Reminiscences of Friedrich Nietzsche (Erinnerungen an Friedrich Nietzsche) op.cit. p. 91ff.
84 Nietzsche's letters to Peter Gast, op.cit.
85 From the posthumous material of the 1880's—(III, p. 835.)
86 From the posthumous material of the 1880's—(III, p. 835.)
87 From the posthumous material of the 1880's—(III, p. 550.)
88 From the posthumous material of the 1880's—(III, p. 635.)

89 Beyond Good and Evil—(II, p. 601.)
90 Twilight of the Idols—(II, p. 997.)
91 From the posthumous material of the 1880's—(III, p. 427.)
92 From the posthumous material of the 1880's—(III, p. 609.)
93 From the posthumous material of the 1880's—(III, p. 599.)
94 From the posthumous material of the 1880's—(III, p. 423.)
95 The Antichrist—(II, p. 1200.)
96 The Antichrist—(II, p. 1196.)
97 Ecce Homo—(II, p. 1092.)
98 The Case Wagner—(II, p. 913.)
99 Letters—(III, p. 1258.)
100 Letters—(III, p. 1138.)
101 From the posthumous material of the 1880's—(III, p. 773.)
102 E. F. Podach, Nietzsche's Collapse (Nietzsche's Zusammenbruch), Heidelberg 1930, p. 77.
103 Letters—(III, p. 1350.)
104 Letters—(III, p. 1350.)
105 E. F. Podach, op.cit. p. 109.
106 P. Deussen, op.cit. p. 96.

BIBLIOGRAPHY

Nietzsche's works in English translation

1 Beyond Good and Evil *(Vintage)*

2 Birth of Tragedy and Genealogy of Morals *(Doubleday-Anchor, 1956)*

3 Joyful Wisdom *(Ungar)*

4 Philosophy in the Tragic Age of the Greeks *(Regnery-Gateway, 1962)*

5 Schopenhauer as Educator *(Regnery-Gateway, 1965)*

6 Thus Spake Zarathustra *(Dutton-Everyman; Modern Library; Penguin, 1961; Regnery-Gateway; Viking-Compass, 1966)*

7 The Use and Abuse of History *(Bobbs, Merrill-Liberal Arts, 1957)*

8 Nietzsche: An Anthology of His Works, ed. by O. Manthey-Zorn *(Washington Square Press, 1964)*

9 Nietzsche: Philosophy: Thus Spake Zarathustra, Beyond Good and Evil, Genealogy of Morals, Ecce Homo, The Birth of Tragedy *(Modern Library)*

10 Philosophy of Nietzsche, ed. by G. Clive *(New American Library, 1965)*

11 The Portable Nietzsche, ed. and translated by W. Kaufmann *(Viking, 1954)*

12 Complete works—18 volumes, Ed. Oscar Levy. Limited edition *(Russell, 1964)*

Works about Nietzsche

Bentley, Eric. A Century of Hero-Worship *(Beacon Press, 1957)*

Danto, A. Nietzsche as Philosopher *(Macmillan, 1965)*

Heller, Erich. The Disinherited Mind *(Farrar, Strauss and Giroux, 1957)*

Jaspers, Karl. Nietzsche, translated by C. F. Wallraff and F. J. Schmitz *(University of Arizona Press, 1965)*

Jaspers, Karl. Nietzsche and Christianity *(Regnery, 1961)*

Kaufmann, Walter. Nietzsche *(Meridian)*

Steiner, Rudolf. Friedrich Nietzsche, Fighter for Freedom *(Herman, 1960)*